The Bartending Therapist

By

Jason Harrell

Edited by
Greg Dawless

Acknowledgments

I am a firm believer that no one realizes their dreams in life without the help and guidance of others. A combination of seeking and good fortune has allowed me to be influenced by so many amazing people that this list will not do it justice, but I would like to highlight some of the most important. Brian Jodice has been my best friend and the brother I always wanted, always inspiring me not only to reach for my goals but teaching me how to be a great person along the way. A former teammate, he was the cohost of my first radio show while also putting up with me as a roommate, and the whole time being my confidant. His loyalty, support, and honesty helped shape me into the man I am today. Coach Maurice Jackson showed me the importance of work ethic and how to always find an opportunity to learn and grow no matter the final score. Ed Ezzell, my favorite teacher, always told me he never had to worry about me because he knew I would do great things. Geoff Hart, my first true mentor in television, taught me that what separates the successful is the time they spend after they clock out, and he taught me how to tell a story that resonates and not just show a highlight. Bob Mihalic was a mentor and friend who always gave me his honest opinion and inspired me to chase my dreams. Greg Wine, my spiritual mentor, showed me that if your life is not what you want it to be, then find someone that has what you want and follow their path. Tom Meseroll, my mentor in the magical arts, showed me that true magic is learning how to make the impossible possible and sharing your gift with others to inspire. Jerry Glaser, my spiritual mentor, keeps me present and reminds me daily that it is progress not perfection that will bring you happiness. William Kay is the big brother I always wanted. Jimmie Harrell, my grandfather, passed along the entrepreneurial spirit. Joan Grogan, my grandmother, took care of me as her own. Bill Ruane, my friend and mentor, keeps me focused and advises me daily. Brian Keiser, one of my closest friends, supported my endeavors without any doubt. Matt Pocius, one of my business mentors, opened the doors to the entrepreneurial landscape. Greg Dawless, my friend and editor, although one of my closest friends, never held back any punches. Riaz Patel, a friend who gambled on my talents to help improve the world. Michael Weircinski, my friend and advisor, has helped coach me every step of the way. Lennox Marshall has been one of my best friends and running mates in entrepreneurship. Jonathan Fischer has been the friend who constantly opens my eyes to the mysteries of the universe and all its power. Akil Leacock has been the friend and producer of the soundtrack to my life. Kevin Holden is the friend that always represented. The list could go on and on, so to all of those whom I have not mentioned here, I will thank you when I see you next, but know that you have helped shape me in many ways, and for that I am grateful.

Finally, my parents who always told me to do what makes me happy. At an early age they showed me how large this world truly is and how little time we actually have in this existence. I am truly blessed to have two loving parents who I can also call my best friends. Their pride in me never stemmed from achievements but effort, and their unconditional love was the fuel that drove me even in my darkest hours. A thank you falls well short of the overwhelming gratitude I have for them. They had one dream for me and gave me a simple goal in life: do what makes you happy, so the best way I can help them realize that dream is to live my life with that mindset.

Introduction

Just about every single person who is of age, and even some cunning individuals with the means and wherewithal to slip through the cracks (you know who you are), has, at one point in their lives, ventured into a bar. I have called the bar home for more than half of my life. The first time I can vividly recall entering a bar was at the tender age of seven in Atlantic Beach, NC, with my parents. Although this may seem abnormal to my peers and the rest of society, I was an only child with an old soul, and my British mother and liberal psychologist father saw no reason to shelter me from life and all it had to offer. I had already played pool in many pool halls with my uncle, and this particular bar in which my parents had frequented in their courtship offered such an opportunity. Times were different and laws not as strict, so a simple nod from the doorman was all that we needed to walk in. There was no real concern that I would be sneaking drinks at that age.

It was a late night, and the liquid was flowing like the waves crashing mere steps away on the sand. I did not even notice how crowded and raucous the joint had become as I played pool with my parents and they enjoyed a few beverages themselves. There was a bit of a commotion nearby, and as I turned from the table to look, barely waist high, I got an eye-level close-up exhibition of a man flashing his prized possession for all to see. He was soon asked to leave, and the night moved on as if this were commonplace. Many might have considered such an occurrence to be a scarring moment in their lives, but, quite the contrary for me, I would later be able to relate this incident to my own personal actions as an adult. There were more than a few times in my early adulthood that after a few beers I would find it necessary to disrobe in public; however, I avoided doing so in bars—I preferred rugby parties.

We all have our first memories of attending a bar, although most stories probably do not include an exhibitionist. What I remember most was how everyone seemed to be having such a great time, and while I now know I was young and naive, the majority of bar goers would probably agree that this basic image rings true for them as well. People go to bars to have good times, and many do—or so they believe. There is no use in trying to quantify the validity or assign a percentage of bar goers who actually have a "good time." After years of experience in bars and behind a few, I have found that there is a good amount of individuals who are fooling themselves about having a good time, as we will discuss in later chapters.

Despite most states' legal age of 21 to purchase or consume alcohol, throughout my youth I found myself in bars. I was 17 when I got a hold of the first of many fake IDs thanks to a trip to NYC. But even before that magical piece of laminated paper, I was able to go into bars with my uncle and enjoy the frosty beverages and social aspects of a bar. My parents and uncle allowed me to drink and taught me how to be responsible, which held true until I attended college. I had friends like most who would binge drink in barns and house parties, but I always remembered the lesson I had learned and would avoid the embarrassment of being drunk on most occasions.

In my later teen years I always befriended those who were older. From the time I first went into a bar I was always accepted, despite my youth. I handled myself well and usually better than the older patrons. I felt a need to be a responsible drinker because I did not want the privileges of going to bars to be lifted. I loved being in bars because I felt mature and accepted. There were times when people would question it, but it must have been evident that I was "cool."

There is something magical about entering a bar, a rite of passage if you will. As a young man being able to saddle up to the bar meant that I was being treated like an adult. This was important to me, and as an old soul I felt more at home there than with my peers sneaking booze and chugging in a back alley or deserted park late at night. Something else occurs that most may not realize when you take your seat at the altar. To me it was like church and receiving communion. As a lapsed catholic I never took to the faith, but I had found my own church in the bar. I use the word "altar" because when you think about it, a bar is structured just like a church. People congregate for many reasons—socializing being the most common—but the reality is that they just want to drink. Just like taking your seat in a pew, you feel at home. You may not know the person on either side of you, but you already have something in common, and it's inviting. In front of you stands an array of spirits arranged judiciously. Your attention is focused, and the bartender, much like a preacher, guides your practice of worship and directs your future, at least for the time spent. You seek everything from the bartender, much like the preacher. Guidance, friendship, and service are provided for a mere token of your appreciation, a tip. Can you see how the tip is much like the donation basket being passed around? Consider the word "spirit" for a moment. One reason it is called such dates back to the early North American trading among the natives. Alcohol was called "spirit water" because it was believed by the natives that upon consumption one would be able to see the spirits of ancestors and the gods. Trust me, if you drink enough you will definitely see some things that are not there; but if you're reading this you probably already have had your own experiences.

I know that many reading this will roll their eyes. As I have found, many people are not regular attendees in church, nor am I; however, the comparison is valid, and what we seek from church is often sought in bars: a sense of acceptance, escape, comradery, and certainly entertainment. My love of bars far exceeds that of church, and I take no issue with calling the bar my church. I have learned many more life lessons applicable there than inside a church. At the age of 24, I would come to find myself taking my position in front of the altar and becoming a bartender. Ironically, despite over a decade of going to bars, I knew that if I were to take this position there would still be much to learn. Just like a preacher goes to seminary school, I enrolled in bar tending school. My first job was in what I consider to be the mecca of bar tending in America: the Big Easy, New Orleans. Some may argue for New York or even Las Vegas, but I will with full confidence put New Orleans bartenders up against anyone. The reason is simple: in other cities there are many occupations that add to those cities' notoriety, but New Orleans has only one reputation, and it is drinking. Tourists have many reasons for traveling. Vegas has gambling as its primary draw. New York is, well, New York—

but New Orleans trumps them all. Certainly there are other aspects that make New Orleans attractive to tourists, but let's be honest, when the most popular street is named Bourbon Street, I think it's a dead giveaway what truly brings them there. I graduated college with a BA in communications but earned my PHD in bar tending and life in the Big Easy.

I had no business jumping into bar tending the way I did, but I was given a shot at a traditional Irish bar called O'Flaherty's just three blocks off of Bourbon Street. Thrown to the wolves, I was finally at home. I was a fast learner, and there was not a cocktail you could throw at me that I could not make while keeping up with conversations and doing math all at the same time. Bartenders are master multitaskers, and during the rush, it's imperative to sling the drinks and handle the money quickly and efficiently. However, the most important lesson that I learned was that in order to be a great bartender you have to wear many hats, and none more important than a therapist. Patrons appreciate a great cocktail and prompt service, but they keep coming back because of the connection and trust they have in their bartender.

My father was a professor and clinical psychologist. I was always interested in his profession, so it makes sense that I would become a bartender. My grades in the few psychology courses I attended were decent, but following in his footsteps never was not an option I wanted to pursue. I wanted to find my own path and in doing so it seemed that the road less traveled was just a parallel to my father's path. I want to state that by no means do I consider myself a psychologist despite my knowledge and experience with the subject matter. I leave that responsibility to my father and those who choose to spend their time becoming licensed. With that said, many are turned off by the counsel of professionals for various reasons, and thus they come to me as their sounding board and counsel. Bartenders have a responsibility at times to play this role, and it is of their own choosing whether or not they act on it when faced with the opportunity or dilemma. There are times at which people open up to me and seek my counsel regarding subjects on which they really should seek professional guidance, and I tell them so. There are other times when I have taken that responsibility and lent an open ear and provided help and insight. This is the purpose of this book. While I am not a professional therapist, the culmination of my own experiences and those who have shared theirs with me has helped me provide for those in need. As a seeker of knowledge I pride myself on self-education and study psychology along with many other subject matters. I am an avid reader who reads close to a book every day. This allows me to be able to cover every topic that's presented across the bar to me. One day I am discussing Elon Musk and Steven Hawking to a SpaceX engineer, and the next day I will talk about the latest sporting acquisitions of the LA Lakers with a journalist from the LA Times. I've held my own with salesmen discussing Oren Klaff's approach from his book *Pitch Anything*, and I've exchanged thoughts with software innovators regarding Peter Thiel and startups. This is one of the areas of being a bartender I take very seriously: know your customers, or whom I like to refer to as "clients." Those who become regulars at my bar are clients. I want to retain their patronage by building rapport and being someone they can relate to. Customers merely buy drinks and move on. But clients are different because they come back for conversation. If I take enough pride in myself to be knowledgeable in a wide variety of subjects, I can create clients, and, when I do, I inevitably become a therapist to them.

Many of you may be wondering where this is all going, but you're interested. You're interested because the all-knowing bartender is an enigma. I am here to pull the curtain and reveal the wizard. We are about to embark on an insightful journey into the psychology of the bar. I have taken the time to break down the different clients who walk through the doors and explain why they come in, become regulars, and what's really going on from my perspective. There are so many questions rattling around when you walk into a bar no matter what the reason happened to be that drew you there in the first place. As a social setting, there is the topic of perspective as it pertains to interaction. Your whole life you have only had one perspective, but as a bartender I have a front row seat to what you are doing right and wrong, your motives and goals. You will find yourself in this book and learn who you are and more about who you are encountering, and maybe who you want to be. I do not stand atop a pedestal and look down on you and pass judgment. This is where you will learn the ins and outs and solve the enigma of the bar and maybe even life. It wouldn't be fair if I didn't pull the curtain on myself and other bartenders so no one is left behind. We will all discover ourselves and each other. I'm taking my guard down, and as you open the door to my literary bar, enjoy! This round's on me.

CHAPTER ONE

What Can I Get Ya?

The first interaction with a bartender is always fascinating to me. The patron approaches the bar big eyed and sometimes even with a sense of confusion about all the options presented to him/her. I always greet them with a friendly "how ya going?" Seems odd, but I picked it up from an Aussie friend of mine years ago, and I do it just to see if they catch on to the slightly different version of "how ya doing?" To this day no one has ever caught on, and this tells me something: they are not really listening. It is not that they are rude; it's simply human nature. We are a self-involved creature prone to missing slight subtleties, especially in this situation. They are consumed with a desire—to get a drink—and never notice this game I am playing. As I grab their order, I gauge whether this is the type of person who's just looking for a drink and a bite and is going to zone out watching the endless loop of *Sportscenter* or someone who is looking to engage. The newbie that is looking for conversation almost always asks the annoying question, "So what do you do or where do you go to school?" It's annoying to every bartender because it assumes that this cannot possibly be one's chosen profession, and we must be pursuing something more. The patron is unintentionally tapping into a common insecurity. Insecurities make anyone uncomfortable or even annoyed, and the reason is because this assumption is correct more often than not. It reminds us that we need to get off our butts and out of the industry. The career bartender is annoyed because it is a slight on his life; they are knocking him without even knowing. The rest of us are annoyed with this confrontation of our insecurity because we are engaged in the pursuit, and while this job may be just a stepping stone, it makes us uneasy about our progress.

For the last decade I have bar tended in the city of Los Angeles, and it's never a surprise to find a wannabe actor, writer, etc. I too can add this to my résumé, and I used to love the question. Like most, I always hoped that my new customer might be a producer or agent and give me my big break. The reality is that this rarely happens, and when it does, it warrants its own Hollywood script. I am no longer annoyed by this interaction and will now let you in on the answer to that inevitable question you may have of me: so what's my story?

As you know I started my bar career in New Orleans, but that was by mere chance. You see every bartender has a story, usually many, and I am no different. I find it humorous when asked if I am in school. It makes me feel like I am young again or at least haven't aged as much as I feel.

I usually respond with, "Nope, I have my degree, and it makes for a great mouse pad."

When I was in college, I pursued a career in sports broadcasting. I began working at the college radio station hosting my own sports talk radio show with my best friend and a format much like that of *Pardon the Interruption* on ESPN. We were doing that format a few years before the show premiered, so we must have been onto something, and I always felt they stole the idea from us. Everyone knows ESPN scouts college radio shows for new ideas, at least that's what we told ourselves. I also worked part-time at a local radio station doing pop radio—

not my finest moment—but I was a god amongst 14-year-old girls. Radio was exciting, but TV was where I wanted to go, and at 19 I accepted an internship at CNN and parlayed it into another internship at TNT on *Inside the NBA*. I spent every day between the two for a summer and even did some reporting that aired across the CNN networks. I continued my internship there, traveling from NC to Atlanta periodically, until I took a position in Ireland at RTE. I was an intern but had many responsibilities and managed to put some stories together for them as well. I graduated college early because I knew my calling and was ready to move on. My first real full-time job in TV took me to Greenville, SC, where I was a sports photographer/reporter/slave.

Channel 6 in Greenville was an amazing experience that taught me so many lessons and skills I use every day. This job was not easy to come by. I had sent over 200 tapes across the country, and no one had called me. I had the resume and talent, but the industry is beyond hard, and the pay is comical. I called the Sports Director, Jack Harris, and told him I would be in the area and would love to sit down with him for lunch and discuss the job. This was a lie; I was back home in NC about six hours away, but I knew in order to get what I wanted I had to be willing to go to any lengths. I think Jack saw this in me, and when he called to tell me I had landed the job, a dream had come true. I moved to SC and made $7.50 an hour working long hours and many times off the clock. I covered every major sport you could name and interviewed nearly every top athlete as well. I was young and on my way, but after two years I felt something turning inside me. I was living below the poverty level, and I was not moving forward like I had hoped. Once again, I would employ the same methods of landing a job, and after 200 more tapes, a dozen interviews, and all rejections, I began to ask myself if there was something more in store for me. I constantly asked myself if I was on the right path. The industry is beyond rewarding. I would walk into my favorite bars and everyone knew who I was—a local celebrity of sorts. They were unaware that every night I went home to a one bedroom apartment with inflatable furniture eating worse than I had in college. Cup of Noodles was a treat and ramen was my savior. I came across a talent agent who knew who I was and took a meeting. She offered me the potential to do modeling and acting as a side income. I jumped at the opportunity, not because I had any major aspirations of being Brad Pitt, but because I just wanted to have some extra money. The opportunities seemed to be worth going for. I did some small projects, and the extra money was nice. I did my first indie film, which never saw the light of day, but it was exciting, and I felt that with my comfort in front of the camera, there may be something to this.

There was a glaring reality that I faced that ultimately became the deciding factor for transitioning out of sports broadcasting. A mentor and friend of mine who was the weekend anchor, Baron, was in his mid-30s, divorced, and bitter. I spent a lot of time with Baron and felt like he was the big brother I had always wanted. In life, everyone can teach you something—sometimes it is what to do and other times it is through an example of what not to do. Baron was successful but bitter about the way his life had turned out. I believed that one day I would work for ESPN, but reality was beginning to set in. ESPN was not the dream job that I had conjured up, and, moreover, the odds of landing there were stacked against me for many reasons that superseded my talent and drive. The reality was that even if I were successful, I could end up like Baron, working every weekend and having long hours that conflicted with relationships, and for little pay. This could be my reality. I could wake up 35 in Middle America, and my job had to be enough to warrant the sacrifice. When I finished my first film, I had a two hour drive ahead of me, and it dawned on me. Life was too short to have a career that encompassed every aspect of my life, and I was only 23. I didn't want to see my 20s rush by with nothing to show for it. I knew that I would not get rich in this industry, but money aside, I knew that I would only have sports related experiences. I traveled a great deal, but I typically would only experience the stadiums and Denny's. There was so much more to life, and I wanted to take the Road Less Traveled. I figured if I ever felt I had made a mistake I could always go back to the industry in some fashion.

I set a jumping off point that gave me three months to allow the universe to help dictate my decision. I still had a few job opportunities across the country. There were three for which I knew I was a top candidate: Myrtle Beach, Des Moines, and Charlottesville. If I were offered a job I would take it, and if not I would be on my way into the new frontier. I interviewed with all three stations, and on a drive back with Baron from a shoot I got the final rejection call. Every opportunity that I had dreamed of had dried up, and I felt completely broken until I remembered what I had told myself.

If none of them panned out, the universe was directing me into a new, exciting direction. Baron could hear the conversation—it was actually Myrtle Beach, the station that had given him his first start in the business.

He said, "Wow, I can't believe they passed. You would have been great for them. Hope it wasn't because of me that you didn't get it."

He had not left on great terms, but I knew he had nothing to do with it. Baron looked at me and noticed I wasn't as dejected as I probably should have been and he inquired, asking if I was okay.

I responded with a question: "Baron, would it sound crazy if I told you I was going to quit and move to LA and try to be an actor?"

He said, "Yeah, I would say that's a little crazy, but you're the perfect age to do it. Don't have regrets. This industry is not just hard to work in but to live in as well. Entertainment is just as hard, but if you break through you will make a lot more money, and if you get rejected you go surfing."

We used to joke and call him "Bitter Baron," but his story is a success, and while he probably never realized how much of a mentor he really was to me, I owe a great deal to him. He later found his calling outside the industry, and while he never made it to the level in broadcasting he had once dreamed, neither did I, and we are so much better for it. He never sugar coated anything, but his opinion was always diplomatic and thoughtful. After that drive I knew that my decision was made, and the next day I put my notice in.

I gave them two months to help get through some of the big events ahead and try to find a replacement. I had no rush and nowhere really to be, but I did have to go home and have the talk with my parents. I came home a week later and sat down with my parents to break the big news.

I am sure that most parents would expect a different conversation: "I am quitting television to do something practical and become a lawyer or something."

This was not their son; I told them being a sportscaster wasn't for me and that I needed something more stable in my life, like being an actor haha.

I have been blessed with the most supportive parents you could ask for, and the first thing my mother said with a smirk was: "You better go to bar tending school first."

Talk about smart—they signed me up once I moved back, and that little certificate has made me way more money than the fancy one from my university. So where does New Orleans come into this picture? Well, while I was enrolled in bar tending school I knew that I needed to save my money up to head west to LA; however, there were plenty of acting opportunities that presented themselves during this process. I did some small gigs for extra money, and an audition came up in New Orleans over 1000 miles away. I had been offered a few days of work on set in Alabama and decided this was once again the universe directing me, so I figured two birds one road trip and headed down south. The filming in Alabama was interesting; it was a reenactment of a civil rights march in Selma. We spent two days filming and marched across the bridge just like the true heroes decades earlier. The money helped cover the travel, but it was an amazing unexpected moment in my life. I could sense the importance of the event we were recreating, and it really took me to that pivotal period in our country's history. Every year I think of that experience on MLK day and am thankful that I was willing to go for it and not listen to the practical voices of a thousand generations that would say it's too far, it's not worth the money, or it's a waste of time.

A bartender's word of advice—"If you have to choose between having an experience or not, don't think of it in terms of money because that experience will likely be invaluable. Make yourself available to be open and welcome it."

After we wrapped, I headed straight for NOLA into the night. All I had was an audition, but, once again, the experience was worth the 2000 mile round trip. I grabbed a crappy hotel and woke up the next morning and headed to the casting office. I was literally there for 15 minutes, in and out. As I hit the road back to NC, I kept thinking, "Wow, I just drove all this way for 15 minutes—what a waste of time." This thought lingered, but then I realized that it was quite the opposite. I was living the dream; a waste of time is sitting at a point in your life without growth or life experiences. I left the TV industry because my life seemed mapped out, filled with routine, and while there would obviously be some cool experiences, they would inevitably be the same type of experiences that would blur over time. As I drove through the backwoods of the South, I found that I was doing exactly what I had intended. I was creating new experiences and stories that would shape my life, stories that I could learn from and later share as I am with you now. I was driving through Atlanta when my phone rang with a NOLA area code.

"Jason, this is Cathy from the casting office. Did I catch you at a bad time?"

"Not at all," I responded.

"Jason, we were really impressed with you today and have a part for you in the film if you would be interested."

"Absolutely!" I didn't even know what the role was or even what the movie was actually about, but what else was keeping me from saying no—hell, they liked me!

"Well, here is the deal, we want you to play a teacher, and filming starts next week. We are going to book you for 21 days of filming over the next four weeks here in New Orleans." Cathy told me of the rate, which by acting standards was not amazing, but I would make almost four times as much as I would in a month as a sportscaster.

I agreed and hung up the phone. Then it set in. I would likely arrive back home late that evening and would have three days to pack up my stuff, find a place to live, and make the long drive back. I called my parents, who were looking forward to my return, and when I informed them of my next move, all they could do was laugh. Of course I would land an acting job and move to a city I knew nothing about while making the decision in a matter of minutes. It wasn't the LA I was expecting but close enough. I came back home and enjoyed the few days with my parents, locked down a sublet for two months, and drove back down. Here is what I did not realize: when you look at a map of New Orleans, it looks like it's right on the ocean, and I had crossed a long bridge across a huge area of water so I assumed if this didn't work out, at least I would be living at the beach. THERE IS NO BEACH IN NEW ORLEANS! I felt so stupid; the water was

Lake Pontchartrain, and the other area of water was the Mississippi River. The closest beach was more than an hour away. But I didn't go there for the water, I went there for the experience. I had to meet with Cathy and sign some papers before filming that Monday. I walked in ready to go when Cathy approached me with a look of despair.

"Jason, so good to see you, but I have some bad news. There has been a change in casting, and we're going to need you to play a student rather than a teacher and only book you for 14 days."

This was a bit of a blow, but I shrugged it off, and a meeting was set later that week to sign another set of papers. Talk about Deja Vu, I walked in that Friday after an amazing week exploring the city, and Cathy had that look on her face again.

"Jason, I have some good and bad news. The director took one look at you and wanted to cast you in a bigger role; however, you will only be filming for five days. The good news is you will be credited, make a little more money, and share some screen time with one of the leads."

This time I was not as nonchalant, but what could I do; I had already moved there, so I agreed, signed some paperwork and looked forward to my role as a police officer. When I got home I realized this was an opportunity. I had paid for two months of rent and had all this free time but little money. I decided that I would put my bar tending school to use and learn the trade. What better place to do so then in the Big Easy? I was disappointed at first that I would not be able to skip this process and jump straight to being a working actor, but I knew that this was the road of many before me. I set out on Bourbon Street going door-to-door looking for a job behind the bar. The French Quarter is an amazing place at night, full of life, excitement, and debauchery; however, in the mornings it is like the *Walking Dead* and smells equally as unpleasant. I had walked with confidence despite no experience in the industry. I had gone to school—that should be good enough. As I went from bar to bar I was faced with constant rejection until I stumbled into O'Flaherty's Irish Pub. I hadn't given much thought as to working there. By this point all I wanted was a bite to eat and a pint to soothe the constant sting of rejection. As I sat there, a woman chain smoked at the end of the bar slamming double White Russians. She was a pill to say the least, but friendly enough to humor me. I told her my story and that I was looking for a bar tending job.

She laughed and said, "Aren't we all in this city?"

She could have written me off, but in that moment a short charismatic Irish man walked in like he owned the place. He had a huge heart that instantly made you feel like you had a friend in a stranger. His Irish accent filled the room as he introduced himself to me. He asked what I thought of this bar I was sitting in, and I told him how at home it made me feel. It reminded me of the pubs I had frequented in Dublin when I lived there. The woman at the end of the bar interjected and said, "Danny, this guy is looking for a bar tending job here in the Quarter. Got any advice for him?"

Danny chuckled and invited me to sit down at a table off in the corner. As I sat down he asked if he could look over my résumé, which I obliged.

After five minutes he looked up at me and said, "You don't even have enough experience to work the door here in the Quarter, much less bartend. Why do you think anyone should hire you?"

18

I felt his words weigh on my confidence like a ton of bricks, but I had been in this situation before, and after a moment I looked him straight in the eye and said, "You're right, I don't have the experience. What I do have is an amazing work ethic and ability to learn faster than anyone I know. If nothing else, people will want to sit at my bar because people love watching sports, and as you can see with my background, there aren't many people that are going to have the stories I can share or the knowledge to speak intelligently about the subject matter. Isn't that the real reason people come to bars, to socialize and connect?"

Danny nodded slightly and asked if I knew who he was.

Of course I had no clue and responded, "No sir, but you look like someone I should listen to."

"That is the most honest answer I could have expected and at the same time insightful," he said. "This place is mine, and I have owned it for 20 years. I opened this place because I play music, and I wanted to bring a piece of my homeland in Ireland here while being able to share my music whenever I wanted to. You have two things going for you: you lived in Ireland and look Irish (which I am), and you remind me of myself. You are not here to just bartend and pay the bills are you? This is a path you need to take to achieve greater goals in your life, and I admire that and want to help. Come back tomorrow and we will fit you in the schedule. Oh, how's your Irish accent and jig?"

Shocked by what had transpired, I drove home talking to myself in an accent and thinking what in the hell he meant by a jig. I returned the following night and began my first day behind the bar. It was an amazing experience, and I never once felt overwhelmed. Many people in the bar industry will tell you that bar tending school is for suckers and the only way to become a bartender is to work your way up. I can agree with this statement; however, I highly recommend bar tending school as long as you take it seriously and try to really study all the cocktails and skills they provide. I had no issues that first day, and for the most part I have never been in over my head behind the bar. I was as good as my fellow bartender that night, but the unexpected happened that I was not prepared for. Danny was playing his Irish music in the bar that night when he paused and called me up on stage.

"This is Jason, a true Irishman, and he is going to do his best Michael Flatley River Dance impersonation."

Anxiety rushed through my body as I nervously laughed; I had never once done a jig but recalled seeing the advertisements years ago. As he began to play, I stood like a deer in headlights, frozen.

Danny yelled at me, "Show us what ya got!"

Startled, I had no choice and began dancing a jig as everyone cheered me on. Danny thanked me as I, sweaty and glad to be finished, walked off stage to everyone's cheers. The patrons came up to me throughout the night praising my skill, and the tips showed their appreciation. That night I made more than a week's wage as a sportscaster, but I also realized an important lesson: act as though you know what you're doing or saying. If you have the confidence behind you, people will believe that what they see or hear is real. This lesson I had not realized was cultivated from my broadcasting days. The myth is that sports guys know everything, but we really don't. Sure, we watch and know more about sports than most, but there are always weak areas (like NASCAR for me). However, when I spoke on the subject I had always done my homework to get me through the segment, and when I would meet people based on this, they would assume I was knowledgeable. Today if you are ever in a situation in which you are not sure of something and have a free moment, GOOGLE IT! I didn't have that luxury back then, but today I utilize it constantly. Fake it till you make it, and the reality is, if you do it long enough, people will believe you, and moreover you will also learn it, even if it is by accident. So here I was, honing my skills as a bartender, dancing a jig, and fulfilling the stereotype of the bar tending actor.

Why did I share this with you? It's simple: every bartender does have a story to tell, and there are many more that I will share with you as we move forward. As I divulge how I became the bartending therapist, just imagine you are sitting at my bar, your home away from home. My clients are usually amazed when they hear my tales, because they are unassuming. Escape is one of the reasons why we frequent bars on business trips. We want to be entertained to some extent, but many bartenders have stories that everyone can relate to and learn from. The worst case scenario is that you will at least be entertained by them, because from my own experiences they are comical. The bartender represents the person who many of us have wanted to be but took the safer, more secure path. There is envy in the bartender when it comes to the money they make for some, but for most it's the lifestyle. I am not exclusively talking about the party at work or the late night rendezvous with the opposite sex, but rather the freedom. We have a job that allows us to pursue something greater. We will

dive more into the bartender lifestyle and path later.
For now, we will continue on how I became who I
am today and how we can learn from the
bartender's perspective about the psychology of the
bar itself and how we can use these lessons in our
lives to grow and understand life on life's terms.

*A bartender's word of advice—"If you fake it
till you make it, eventually you won't have to fake it
anymore."*

CHAPTER TWO

Katrina, What a Bitch

In New Orleans, being an actor/bartender is special. The aforementioned questions that bartenders find annoying are typically not annoying when we are starting out. The question of whether I was in school was warranted, since I barely shaved and looked like Harry Potter despite being ten years older.

When approached with the question of school and if I was working my way through school, I countered with: "No, I graduated and worked as a sportscaster, but now I am an actor."

This caught many off guard because they did not realize this was even an option for someone in New Orleans. But at this time, the industry was booming in the city, and it proved to be a good launching point not only to break into the industry with less competition, but to hone my skills behind the bar so that when I made the trek out west, I would be skilled and able to survive.

This combo was a surprising treat to tourists. They did not expect to be served by a potential movie star since they were not in LA or NYC. It created interest, and the conversations were compelling and kept the drinks flowing. The reality is that I was actually a bartender first, and most are somewhat delusional of this fact. You work fulltime and pay the bills with this job, which is a great complement to your pursuit of the career you are chasing. Bartending was my job, but acting was my career at this time. I was becoming comfortable at this point making more money behind the bar than I had ever seen while working constantly, jumping from project to project, hoping for that big break and magic carpet ride to LA. The universe had other plans in store, as the worst natural disaster to hit the USA in modern history loomed on the horizon. I was working on a film as Brendan Fraser's stand in and had been booked for weeks on the film. I had made contacts and a good impression. The director took notice and had promised me a speaking role, which would guarantee me a SAG card, the first step to being a working actor. It was the last week of my stand in duties, and a role was in place for me the following week when the reports came in. It was Friday when we were told to halt production because of the impending hurricane. What people do not realize about Katrina is that the buildup was nonthreatening, and the locals had no fear. The fishbowl of a city had many jokes concerning the big hurricane that was destined to flood the city but over 50 years with so many close calls there was an arrogance and no one was making plans of evacuation.

I was so excited for my filming opportunity that I adopted this nonchalant arrogance of the locals, and two days before it was expected to hit, I began to seek plans for finding a hotel and possible hurricane parties. This was the mindset and reality of the city just 48 hours before our lives would change forever. I was not the only one with this great idea, as all the hotels were sold out. My plan altered, and I decided to park my car in a garage and ride the storm out at the bar enjoying the powers of nature and partying till the last drop. Sunday morning I was alarmed by a bang at the door and found the police on the other side. They informed me that I had one hour to evacuate or else they would take me to the Superdome. With only an hour, I called my only fellow NC friend in the city, Kathy, and we decided to drive west to find a hotel until we could come back. As I lightly packed, I watched the reports. At the time, Katrina was barely a hurricane, and so I packed a two day bag of clothes, my Xbox to play in the hotel, and my suits for some reason. I picked up Kathy, and we joked about the overreactions by the city. You have to understand, the locals had heard countless cries of wolf and were hell bent on staying. I did not want to go to the Superdome, so we hit the road. If you have ever seen an apocalyptic film, we were living it. It was called "contraflow," and once we were in it, there was no turning around. The 10 freeway was going in one direction and there were no exits. It was beyond a traffic jam, and we spent 12 hours driving to Lafayette a mere 45 miles away. We were lucky and found a hotel for the night and took refuge. Kathy was nervous, as we had both experienced major hurricanes in our given times in NC, but rather then worry I sought out the hotel bar. Everyone was glued to the TV, and the party was actually exciting. The projections were catastrophic, but by the time I went to bed, I was convinced that this would just blow over and I would be back in a day or two. Everyone felt the same way as I went to bed, drunk as a skunk. I took solace in this notion. Eight in the morning my phone rang, and my mother was hysterical asking me where I was. Light heartedly I joked and told her I was in my bed, where else would I be? She screamed, "Get out of bed and leave right now! This is the big one."

I had refrained from telling her the day before that I was leaving, but I filled her in to her relief and turned on the TV.

"Category 5, New Orleans will crumble!" The

news rocked me to the bone as I saw this was not going to blow over and our worst fears would be realized. I watched the coverage to the point of impact because there was nothing to report until it was over. The following morning I was awakened by a phone call from the front desk informing me that if I wished to extend my stay it would be $400 a night, nearly four times the amount we had been paying. We had one hour to check out as we returned to see the aftermath of Katrina. Reports were inconclusive at the time, and there was no entry allowed back into the city. The freeway was impassable, and there was no certainty as to what we would have to return to, if anything.

We made the decision to drive back to NC and hit the road after checkout. As we drove north without knowledge of the degree of wreckage, an unsettling reality overcame Kathy and me. We would not be going back to New Orleans for some indefinite time. We reached Monroe and grabbed a bite and filled up on gas. This proved to be a wise decision as we drove through Alabama and Mississippi. There was no power, no radio stations, and no certainty if we would even make it home. As we crossed in to GA we were almost out of gas and had one last hope of filling up or being stranded. Our good fortune continued as we pulled in and found the gas station equipped with power and able to save us from destitution. The attendant informed us that they were one of the few that maintained power and the states we had just left were completely devastated and had no power. We pressed on and made it back to NC, I dropped off Kathy at a truck stop where her parents met us. This was the last time I ever saw her, and this would be the case of nearly everyone that I had befriended in New Orleans. I came home exhausted and greeted by my parents who were so happy to see me—I had dodged a bullet that I never really believed was coming. I slept through the night and awoke refreshed, but this was the beginning of a long day. As I sat on the couch curled up like a small child, I watched with tears coming and going as the reports came in. Everything I knew about the city was wiped away like raindrops on a windshield. This was before the overwhelming presence of cell phones and social media. Myspace was in its infancy; in fact, I wasn't even on it at the time. There was no way to reach out and see who was alive or safe. It was the most heart wrenching day of my life to that point.

What people do not know about those who went through Katrina was that the relief effort was actually staggering. People questioned why so many stayed, but they did not know their history as I have shared. I can agree that there was unbridled arrogance that proved costly but history had shown that New Orleans was always spared. In fact, at the last minute Katrina did what all hurricanes approaching the city had done in the past and turned inward into the panhandle; only this time, the hurricane was too large to miss the city completely. At one point bands were hitting Chicago as well as NOLA at the same time. The way it grew overnight was projected but not expected, and that's why people stayed. I felt I did not have much of a decision to stay and was lucky to benefit from it. The other myth was that help was not sent in a timely manner, but I can attest to the hundreds of military trucks I passed leaving Louisiana. I assume they simply had no way of entering the city. I can agree that the preparation was subpar by all measures, but it's hard to prepare for a once-in-a-lifetime occurrence, so it angers me when I hear of the ignorance that comes from hindsight on this tragedy. I despised those who tried to console me by saying, "Everything happens for a reason."

It took me years to realize this was true, but it did little for me to feel better faced with not knowing if my friends were dead or alive. Even as I write this, I do not know who made it or not, but I have to use that lack of knowledge to fuel me to live, for those who paid the ultimate price. I am no longer a Katrina victim but a survivor.

It took me a few years to truly grasp that mindset. I fell into a deep depression and self-medicated with alcohol, as one might expect. There was a moment in which I found myself after a night of drinking with a friend at his beach house standing at sunrise at the end of a pier. There was no one within sight, and my depression had full control over my life and psyche. The pain was unbearable. Everything I had worked for was ripped away with no reason, and I cursed God for this. As I stood at the rail I flung my legs over the edge and sat there looking at the cold water. I did not want to kill myself, but I didn't want to feel this pain nor did I know how I could go on carrying it with me through life. I made the decision that if I jumped in and made it to shore that would be God's will for me to live. If I died, then that was my destiny. I was full of fear when a soft voice came from seemingly nowhere.

"Ya know son, that water looks pretty cold down there. It's probably safer on this side of the rail."

As I looked behind me, an old fisherman stood there with his pole and bucket full of bait. He could see the pain in my eyes but stood stoic. For what seemed like forever, I looked into his eyes, then nodded my head as I pulled my legs to safety and stood there. He gave a slight smile and turned to prepare his hook for his first cast of the day. Christians may say that this was divine intervention, maybe even Jesus given he was a fisherman. To this day I do not know how to quantify this experience, but I have always felt that someone was looking out for me and that day he came in the form of a fisherman. I said nothing and walked back to my friend's beach house and fell asleep.

When I woke up, I was filled with promise and was no longer going to let this pain rent space in my head any longer. I thanked my friend for the good times and headed back home. An hour on the road and my phone rang. It was my friend Ken, who was a fellow bartender from New Orleans at a local spot I frequented. We were not that close, but both of us rejoiced in finally hearing from someone who had made it out and being able to reconnect. We talked for a few minutes trying to track down who we knew and if they had survived. Finding much needed companionship in this time of need, we turned our conversation to a positive note.

"What now?" Almost instantaneously we asked this question.

He had known of my acting aspirations and how I was going to move to LA at some point. He had spent some time there and was in the music industry. In an instant a decision just like so many before was made. We would head to LA together and start anew. I would hit the road the day after Christmas with the expectation of making it to LA for the New Year. I had a purpose and drive that had been sidetracked in New Orleans. Sometimes moderate success can overshadow the larger picture. I had become comfortable in New Orleans and my plan to head to LA had faded away. But now, now it was back and back with a vengeance. I had lost everything in one fell swoop, and while this can hold many people back with fear that it could happen again, I was no longer going to be the story of what could have been. Fear is defined by some as False Evidence Appearing Real. I would live for those I had lost. I was stronger because I knew what it was like to be at the bottom and get back up and push forward. It was time to get to work knowing that if I lost everything again and LA didn't work out, I would still survive. I don't wish a Katrina on anyone in their life, but if you go through something like this, it can be your greatest strength. As I look back on it, that tragedy is why I succeed today. As it is said, every great story begins with failure or tragedy, and the day after Christmas in 2005 was the first chapter in mine, and everything else to this point was simply the prologue.

A bartender's word of advice—"Everything does happen for a reason, but many times it will not be revealed until you find a set of glasses that provide a clear perspective."

CHAPTER THREE

Coming to LA

It was the night of Christmas day as I sat with my parents in front of the warm fire just like years past. Maybe there was an element of drama I was trying to create by leaving the day after Christmas, but to me it made sense. I couldn't wait till the right time or tomorrow, I had to move forward in my life today. A few months had passed from the day at the pier, and since that day I had worked more ferociously than I ever had in my life. I found a job as a server during the day, then went to my next job bartending at a country club, and after closing, I would DJ at a local bar until 3am. Any opportunity to make money and save I jumped at it because my dream was as important as breathing. I was not clear on what my dream exactly was. Was it to be a successful actor or would my life take a different direction? The dream was not about an end goal but rather a journey. My dream was to start the journey toward something great and live a life like it was my last day. Many say this but never truly embrace it. There have been days that I forgot this idea, but I always remember that I was not promised anything in life, especially tomorrow, and Katrina had taught me this lesson.

If you want to make God laugh tell him your plans. I had a plan when I moved to New Orleans and had become sidetracked and then completely derailed. This was the God shot that I needed to get back on track. It would be very narcissistic to say that the reason Katrina happened was solely to move me forward, but that was the mindset I needed to adopt. Certainly Katrina affected millions, but I am not responsible for their lives nor do I live their lives; I live my own. This was my motivation, and as I sat in front of the fire I could sense my family's concerns, but there was assurance that they believed in me and fully supported my pursuit. In order to find something more you have to prepare, but even more so, you have to put yourself in position to receive it, and driving across the country was the first step. To say the success story was simply pulling out of the driveway would not be true. It was the first step, but life is not that easy, and there were many challenges that lay ahead. The last conversation I had with my parents before I left was a serious one.

"We support you, Jason, and believe in you, but you must understand that we cannot help you. You will have to do it on your own. The best we can offer is a flight home in case you fail," my parents told me.

This was hard to hear. I respect them for this because it was the first time in my life I was truly stepping away from any safety net. I was making a decision that in the end I would have to rely on myself to navigate any troubles or obstacles that lay ahead. I was nervous but overwhelmed with excitement. I have never jumped out of a plane, but I would like to think that the two are synonymous. I was standing at the edge knowing that I had to pull the cord in order to land safely and no one else would be there to help. That immense fear drove me, and in order to achieve great rewards, the risks would have to be just as high. This is true, but I had a secret weapon. I had felt the bottom, and while I didn't like it, I knew it wouldn't kill me, and that knowledge allows you to go for it. In the movie *Fight Club* it is said that once you have lost everything you are free to do anything. I was free, and with Whitesnake's "Here I Go Again" blasting at full volume, I pulled out of the driveway ready to face all of my fears and enter the world as a survivor, not as a victim.

I told you there would be obstacles, and the first came before I even made it through Texas.

My phone rang, and it was Ken: "Jay, I'm not gonna meet you in LA just yet. I need to save more and meet you out there, but my friend Carl said you can crash with him until I get there."

This was not as crushing as I would have thought but rather made the journey more exciting. I was angered at first but remembered that I was all in, on my own, and couldn't rely on anyone. This was just a reminder of that notion. When I arrived in LA, the city was everything I dreamed of and seemed to stretch on forever. I connected with Carl, and he welcomed me in as if we had been childhood friends. He was a Nigerian who had battled cancer in his youth and was a fighter. We were exactly what each other needed in our lives at that moment and pushed each other. I reminded him why he was in LA and motivated him to get back in the game. He had been caught up in the rat race of survival, and now he had an example of someone who was going to push forward no matter what, which reminded him of his fight against cancer. I slept on an inflatable mattress in his living room for three months until Ken arrived. It was humbling, but I was in a place of gratitude and never once took pity on myself. I jumped into work mode right away, landing a few acting gigs similar to the ones I had had in New Orleans and found a job bartending at a wine bar in downtown LA. It was not ideal since I lived on the West side and traffic could make my commute close to an hour, but it was a start. Ironically, I would unwillingly make it harder on myself from the get go.

It was early February when I met up with a girl I didn't really know for a night out in Hollywood. I had been in bars half my life, and that night was no different as we went out to enjoy the full Hollywood scene. We bar hopped the Sunset Strip, going to every bar I had read about: The Viper, The Rainbow, Whiskey a Go Go, and finally the Key club...I think. I was doing what most would do when they are new, keeping up. What I didn't realize is that the group I was introduced to by this girl didn't seem to be as affected by the amount of booze we were annihilating. I had always had a high tolerance, but could not keep up. I later realized cocaine does an amazing job of keeping you level, but I wasn't aware of it and had never been into that scene. As we arrived back at her place, the night had become a blur, but I do remember having a gut feeling that this was not going to end up well. There was an argument that I have no recollection of, and my instincts told me to leave since I did not know them well. I left the apartment and found my car with full intentions of passing out. After lying there I made the decision that I could drive.

To this day I don't remember many details, but one memory stands out—I was sitting on the curb with my face in my hands. I recall saying over and over again, "My life is over." I had gone down the wrong way of a one-way street and had gotten into a head-on collision. No one was hurt, thank God, but I was taken to jail, where I would spend the next three days until I posted bail and was released. It was the hardest phone call I ever had to make to my parents, and it was from jail. Their worst fears had been realized: I had jumped out of the plane, and my chute didn't open. I had landed flat on my back. I say on my back and not my face because I had survived and did not die. That would have been the worst, but God gave me an opportunity to rise again. This was not like Katrina; I was not a victim. I had placed myself in this situation all on my own. Sure, there were moments of "why me" and of having a pity party, but it quickly subsided because I knew I didn't have time to waste.

Once back at Carl's, I phoned my parents, and they gave me two options: I could join the military (that had been my father's solution when he had gotten a DUI), or I could head to LAX and fly back home to start over.

As tears ran down my face, I sat there silent awhile before finally saying, "No, I will take the third option."

They were miffed and argued that there was no third option and this was the only way they could help. I reminded them of the night in front of the fire when they told me they wouldn't be able to help me and I would be on my own. The fire now lay ahead, and I would have to walk through it. I know they wanted to believe in me, but their doubt was evident and I could sense it, despite their support. They wanted to save me, and I love them for that, but in order to truly save someone, you have to let them stand on their own. This was rock bottom. I had no money because my savings went to my lawyer. I had no car in a city that makes it damn near impossible to survive without one, but I broke out my tool belt and got to work. I went to a bike shop and financed a 300 dollar bike. That's right, I FINANCED it at 10 bucks a week which sounds hilarious to me now. I would ride a bike and make it. I told you I would make it difficult, and to everyone who hears my story, this situation might be better described as impossible. I am here to tell you that nothing is impossible, and I am living proof.

I rode my bike to downtown LA for my bar tending job. If there was an acting gig, no matter where it was I found a way to get there, and if there was an audition I packed a bag. I was like superman walking into Starbucks in my bike clothes and then emerging as a well-dressed actor moments later. I had an improv class that was in the valley 25 miles away through the Sepulveda pass, which twists its way through the Hollywood hills. I made that ride every week until a fellow student realized what I was doing and began to give me rides. I ate one dollar TV dinners and my only luxury was a three lb bag of M&Ms that were on sale on Wednesdays at the local Ralph's. I found a job writing for an internet news station that I could do from home, and the journey was still in progress. With the DUI penalties I tacked on 200 hours of community service, a DUI program, and AA meetings. I made a decision that I could not afford drinking anymore, and since it had gotten me into the situation in which I found myself, it would be wise to refrain in order to survive. When people tell me they can't do something or afford something, I ask them to really look deep down as to why. It is the sacrifices that we must be willing to make that will get us to our goals as long as our goals are worth the fight. That comes from a place that most people are unwilling to seek. They are unwilling to compromise because it's too hard or scary. I embraced it, and when Ken arrived three months later, he rightly had his reservations about me. What he quickly saw when we were reunited was that I was no longer the same guy he had befriended in New Orleans. I was stronger and more reliable than he or even I could have imagined.

The Last Hurdles until the Next Race

When Ken arrived he was not content with having summer camp in Carl's living room. He parked his inflatable mattress next to mine, but we would have to find a place in short order. I was beyond struggling financially, but I was making headway. He had prepared well and had a good nest egg. We found a place and moved into a two bedroom in West LA. This was a big step, and after moving everything in, I felt I was unstoppable. However, the universe has a funny way of making you right sized in a hurry. Sitting on the couch with big smiles and feeling like we had made it, I was optimistic. I was still riding my bike, but I had two decent jobs and could afford the rent. Then the phone rang, and the first blow came. It was the bar downtown, and the owner addressed me with concern. She informed me that the bar was not doing so well and that they were cutting staff. This was tough to hear, but there was nothing I could do. I wasn't terribly worried because the news job would provide enough to get by until I got another bar gig. I didn't get laid off because of anything I had done; it was just the circumstance, and I was accepting. Just like a boxing fight, it is the jab that sets up the hook—it was coming for me, and I was blindsided. An hour later the phone rang again. It was my producer at the Internet news show. He regretted to inform me that they didn't get the support or funding to continue and that they would call me if something changed, but for now I was out of work. With 70 dollars in my bank account and 30 days to pay the rent, I was crushed.

Sitting there in disbelief, I had no answers and was static. I couldn't believe how the last year had gone with so many ups and downs. I felt that they were mostly downs but something was different. There is a progression that I now see, and it was key to my growth. I did not sulk or throw a pity party this time. Instead, I got straight to work and scoured the Internet looking for opportunities. I had a meeting the next day with my lawyer that went well, and I would avoid any further jail time for my actions. The judge had shown me mercy, and for the first time there was some relief in my life, albeit small. There was a restaurant next door to the law office that was right on the water and something told me to seize the opportunity and never waste a moment. I needed a job, and there was none too small because I had rent to pay. I walked into this rustic place called The Waterfront and asked to speak to the manager. As luck would have it, they had just posted an ad that day, and here I was. Because of my New Orleans experience, they told me to come back the next day to start training as one of their bartenders had put in his notice, and they needed to fill the position right away. I trained for two weeks and was given the crappy shifts, but it was a start.

I knew immediately during my training that this job would work for me, but I would not be able to make the rent on time. I took some odd jobs, even handing out flyers to comedy shows, anything to put cash in my pocket. One night, still pursuing the acting scene, I came across a last minute call that was paying $1200. I knew there was something odd about this gig, and when I read the details I found the reason. They needed six males the next day to be able to film full frontal. I looked at this ad and all I could do was laugh. This was the epitome of a Hollywood story. It was not porn but rather a show on the IFC network. What would my parents think? Could I really go through with it? I could now understand why people did porn or nudity in their early acting careers; it's tough out there. If you are hungry you will do anything to eat, and I was right there. I submitted myself and was called minutes later. They gave me my call time, and I rode my bike to the set the following day.

I was greeted by a PA who chuckled at me and said, "Man you've got some balls, haha, and now everyone's gonna see them."

I smiled and nodded as I followed him to sign in. I was flooded with nerves and the potential embarrassment I could possibly face that day and for a lifetime. I felt that this was just another road less traveled that I would have to go down. The producer gathered the six of us and sat us down to brief us on our roles.

"Thanks so much for coming, guys, we truly appreciate your services on this project, but we have to let you guys know some things that will put some of you at ease and two of you at even more ease. First, you will be wearing masks, so the only people that will recognize you will be those that really know what you look like (he said with a wink). Also, we only need four of you; we booked six just in case there were no shows, so we will have a mini audition of sorts and then decide. You will all get the rate, but the two not selected will just hang around for the day as backup."

The director came in and instructed us to stand side by side. I was the tallest of the bunch, and he came over to me first.

"I don't think we can use you; we kinda need everyone to be the same height. Just one question: are you circumcised?"

"No, sir," I replied.

He laughed and said, "Well, it's your lucky day; we can't use you so hang tight and collect your check."

FINALLY, my parents were right—it was better to be uncut! Years of being made fun of in the locker room because my liberal euro parents decided at birth I would not look like every other American boy had paid off. I'm not sure 1200 bucks was enough for the psychological damage, but it worked for me that day. They kept me for four hours and fed me the best meal I had had in weeks. I rode my bike home beaming. Being willing to put yourself out there and do what needed to be done had paid off. I had jumped the last hurdle and made the rent. The next month my new job proved to work out well as I was making enough to cover my nut without having to show my nuts. That was the last time I ever really worried about having enough, and while the journey to that point had tested me in every facet of the word, I had persevered. Now I was on my way.

Now You're a Regular

When I share this story from behind the bar, reactions are varied inside the patrons' heads. I am certain, however, that it is an inspiring tale and that regardless of the size of their tab they have received way more than an entertaining night out. I have let you into my world and made you question the bartender forever. He is no longer just a servant but someone to confide in. The report that has been forged will bring them back time and time again. I hope by this point you have begun to visualize this book as more than a read and now a journey. Imagine you have just finished up your day and sat down at my bar like you have done many times before. We have made our introductions, and now that you know a bit more about me you no longer feel like a stranger but, instead, have found your own version of *Cheers*. This is what the majority of us are looking for: comfort and recognition. I may not always remember your name the next time I see you, but you will remember mine and most likely I'll know your drink before you even ask for it. That's the pride I take in my work. Many times the bartender forgets this notion and does not create regulars. They are too concerned with the life that is being led once they clock out. I can tell you that no matter how large their dreams are, if they cannot put as much effort into their job as their dreams, they will fall short. I didn't set out to become the bartending therapist, but I am paid to provide a service, and anything short of that is not only a disservice to my employer but also a disservice to myself.

It is an investment, and there is no rarer commodity than time. If you were given 86,400 dollars a day to spend but at the end of that day you would lose it all, how much of it would you waste? That is how I look at my time; I can't get it back, so while I have it, I will make the most of it, even when I have to go to my day job. It is because of this discipline and mindset that I can be prepared for success. If I work 40 hours a week without this concept then I will begin to adopt bad habits so that when I go home at night to work on my dreams, they will seep in and cripple me. That is why I take the time to let you in, and when I do that you will do the same. Most are already willing, but if they have confidence that they are speaking to someone of substance then the true magic can take place. We can both grow, making our time together valuable.

I can see a different vantage point of the reader asking, "Why would I want this," or saying, "This is not what I am looking for; I just want to drink and catch the game."

For those in this category, which we will touch on in a later chapter, that is totally acceptable. If that is your goal, I will stand back and allow you to spend your time at your will. BUT what about the time that will one day come, when no one you know will listen to you? Maybe everyone whom you confide in doesn't have the answers, or worse, even an option for a solution. When these doors are closed you may find yourself at the bar. You will know that there is one guy that has been through a lot, and his experiences can prove helpful. That one moment is what I am prepared for, and that's why I share my story willingly. To trust your bartender is not to walk in his shoes, but to know that he has walked many miles in his own and has more to offer than meets the eye. This is not the rule, but it is the practice when I am across that three feet of bar top.

Imagine from here on out that you are saddled up at my bar as we go on. This is not a story but an experience I am about to lead you on that will allow you to envision a way of life through an ecosystem that comes with the bar psychology. You can trust that when I know something that can help, I will share it. It is like I am a coach, showing you the framework that has worked for me. It is up to you to implement it, take it in, and cultivate your own path. Worst case scenario, you will have a friend who's there to listen no matter the high or the low. I don't always have the answers, but I have knowledge that I have utilized over the years from a varying array of experiences and study.

As we move on, you may be saying to yourself, "This guy has quite the story in becoming a bartender, but that doesn't make him credible."

You are right in the sense that there is no certificate or diploma to become a bartending therapist, but ask yourself, "Why do I seek out the bartender and unload on him some of my personal details of my life?"

Maybe this is not you, but then why does your friend, or the guy at the end of the bar, or the coworker seek this guy out?

You know where I come from, but now we will explore why my position is sometimes referred to as the "All-Knowing Bartender." I can only speak for myself and some generalizations of bartenders that I know, but if you're reading this, I would wage a hefty bet that there is no need to convince you of the validity of this moniker. Welcome to the University of Bartending, the school of the real world and self-education!

A bartender's word of advice—"Life is full of obstacles and choices. You will face many decisions and worry about making the right choice. Just remember that the one who stands still may avoid failure or success but has still made a decision."

CHAPTER FOUR

Bartending U (Self Accredited)

There are many stereotypes when it comes to the service industry, and the most frequently encountered stem from education. That question about working our way through school annoys us for one reason: most of us have already been there and done that. In the United States, over 16 percent of bartenders have a bachelor's degree, and while that number is not staggering, I can attest that that number is a lot higher in LA where I work. Every bartender I have ever worked with has at least attended college, and most have degrees. The reason it is annoying is the assumption that we are not educated. The question usually stems from those with degrees; those without seem to appreciate that you have a job, and that is enough for them. For some, they may even be envious if they have an inkling of how much we make.

The perception of education has changed to the intellects of the world. Throughout my life I was bombarded with ads telling me that education was so important and that with a degree I would earn more money, have a better job, and a better life. It is easy for me to question this notion now, especially since I have a degree, but the reality is that times have changed. If I had a child of college age, I wouldn't have the same vision as my parents. It was never a question of if, but where I was going to college. For my generation, it was pivotal, and the evidence was glaring that a degree was a huge advantage. There is an arrogance that comes with earning a degree, and it is not until years later for most that they realize the degree does not entitle you to anything. If you take the top 25 richest people who dropped out of college and compared them to those who earned higher education degrees you may be shocked to find that the dropouts actually made more. Three dropouts come to mind right away and may be worth more combined than the majority of the other list: Bill Gates, Richard Branson, and Mark Zuckerberg.

Formal education is not a way of life but merely a tool. It is not the all-purpose tool we are led to believe it is. So what makes the bartender seemingly so knowledgeable? Let's be honest, with fewer than half actually having degrees, and the ones who do not really using them, why do they bartend and why do they know so much? Here is a secret that we know that I will let you in on: the key is a combination of self-education and exposure. I recall as a child my parents instilled within me the importance of life experience over everything. When I was 14, my parents saved up, and while they probably still could not afford the trip, we went to London and Paris. I was too young and immature to truly appreciate what I was being exposed to, but my memory was sharp enough to record everything I experienced. I had a World History class with Mrs. Malone, who was the worst kind of teacher. It was a small town, so her textbook knowledge of the world made her seem "worldly." She asked if anyone had ever heard of the Rosetta stone one day, and no one raised their hand. A look of superiority came over her face, which was common for all the topics we covered; but this time, before she could shine, I rose my hand. I shrugged my shoulders and said it was a big rock.

She laughed and asked, "Is that all you know about it?"

She bit hook, line, and sinker: "No, it was discovered with an inscription on the tablet that would prove to be the translation of hieroglyphics and help unlock the meanings of the text from the ancient world," I answered.

Sure, I was a bit of a brat in showing her up, but the shock on her face was worth it. The challenge was not over.

"How did you know that?"

"Ha, know it? I've seen it, haven't you?" I smirked.

It was then revealed that she was not as worldly as she would lead us to believe, and while this was no monumental dethroning, what was important was that I learned that experience trumps those that reign superior over the ignorant. I may not know the exact history of the Eiffel Tower, but I can tell you that they sell warmed nuts underneath it not to eat, but to put in your pockets to warm your hands. The line at the Louvre is long as hell, and the Mona Lisa is a bit of a disappointment visually. In the moment I didn't pay much attention to what I was experiencing, but the fact that it was an experience as opposed to a lecture in a classroom impacted me and imprinted on my memory. I do not think less of her because she was actually well read. Her ignorance was not in her knowledge but in the way she wielded it to the unknowing. I think reading is equally as important, and that's why I read so much; however, the way she used this knowledge to act superior was why I challenged her. Was it my place? Was I a brat? I do not know, but it was an important moment in my life in how I value things and do not simply take them for face value. I would rather my child spend a summer backpacking through Europe going to museums rather than a semester taking survey courses in college. Which one do you think will impact him more and thus create a better return on the investment? Most people don't really consider this, but the true sign of an intellect is knowing that there are no right or wrong choices but simply choices. Even when you believe you're right, think about the other side and see if you can argue it; only then will you truly find answers and insight.

Bartenders have more life experiences than most people. Last year alone I traveled to four countries and six new cities in the USA; how many vacations does John Public take working his 9-5? Not too many, which is a shame, not because he doesn't want to but because he cannot. This is why they come to us when they are thinking of traveling. We travel more than most and know where to go, how to get there cheap, and the best bartenders to seek out once you are there (we can smell our own). We have this knowledge because we do it; we don't dream or simply read about it. The bartender works to live and does not live to work. We only live to work when we have a dream that requires this mindset, but the reality is that we love what we are doing, so really it's not a burden and it excites us. As a former actor, I loved my days off because it allowed me to do all the grunt work that goes with the industry. I would have to go to classes, read, and write scripts, put together mailers, go through listings, etc. The list would seem endless, but I never thought to myself, wow, all this "work" sucks, because I was doing what I wanted to do. So while most work one job and learn one thing at minimum, we are learning two things but typically a lot more.

This will sound ridiculous, but let me paint a picture. There is a bartender named Sally who is quite the looker but never went to college. She grew up loving the beach and surfing the waves, and a career was never really a priority. She skated her way through high school, and while everyone else was looking to college she was figuring out a way to move out and live steps from the beach. She wanted to support a life of surfing and traveling in search of the perfect waves across the globe. She worked her way up before becoming a bartender, and by the age of 27 she had surfed six continents, cultivated a perfect tan, and now drives a new car and has a place right on the beach. People actually look down on Sally from time to time thinking that she is wasting her life and wondering what will happen when she is 40 or if she will have a family. That word *perspective* has to come into play.

The reality is that the vast majority of people in this country will not be able to retire and tend to save less than three percent annually. When they have families they tend to be living in debt. Sally has no formal education, but her bills are paid on time, and while there may be a question of what she will do when she is 40, she is in no better or worse position than the people who are questioning her. What's funny is, deep down, these people are envious because they are victims of their own doing and are leading lives that society or maybe even their parents told them they must in order to be "successful." Successful by what measure though? Sally thinks she is successful, and I agree. She has set goals and achieved them even if they are not the ones that society may deem as successful. The one who is questioning may seem successful on paper, but do they have the joy from life that she does? You can decide either way which is the right ideology in this example, but remember the intellect argues both ways. Here is the twist: despite all of what has just been revealed, why do patrons seek her counsel and possibly unintentionally rely on her therapeutic insight? Here is the answer:

When Sally wakes up she flips on the local news to hear the surf report, but while she is waiting for that segment, she is exposed to the news stories of the day, making her knowledgeable about the world around her. After her cup of coffee and breakfast, she hits the waves about the time that you are waking up, which gives her joy and spiritual bliss. It is also a workout, which keeps her healthy. When she comes home she takes care of her daily chores and bills before going into work. The news and sports channels are on all day, and whether she has interest in them or not she is exposed to them all so when someone sits down and asks what the weather will be, did the Dodgers win, or what was that big news story from the day, she knows about it. She converses with some patrons who are doctors, lawyers, and engineers, and they tell her about the news in their industry and how it affects them. More exposure to new information is as constant as the waves she rides, so when you walk in she always has insight and can contribute to nearly any topic thrown in her direction. This is true of nearly every bartender that I know, and ironically it is not because we necessarily have a thirst for the knowledge but more that we are open and available to receive it. This makes us more diverse than the accountant who spends his whole day doing the same thing over and over. The accountant has to seek the information that makes one worldly, while Sally is simply exposed to it due to her daily interactions and way of life.

Sally is the standard, but every now and again

you will walk in to find a bartender like me who not only is exposed, but seeks knowledge for personal growth. As I look up from this text I am faced with hundreds of books I have read. In fact, I read close to a book a day, not for bragging purposes, but for personal growth and a thirst for knowledge. No one sees me reading them nor sees my library, but I do this because that is what successful people do who want more from life. It has proven helpful in solidifying me as an example of the all-knowing bartender. I was talking to an engineer from Spacex one day, and I could sense that while talking about his job, he was used to the subject matter going over people's heads. The reality is that if he goes really in-depth, I would be no different, but I had an array of talking points that he was not accustomed to. One day I brought up his company's founder, Elon Musk, and his work ethic. I was curious to discover if he employed his staff to work the same way. The patron was unaware of what I was talking about, and then I mentioned Stephen Hawking and his findings in his book *A Brief History of Time*. Again, he was befuddled because he had not read his works. We went back and forth having a conversation that would not seem likely, and in the end he shook his head with a smile and asked how I knew so much. I laughed and said I read a book a day. Here was a man who had a PhD from MIT in engineering, and he could not fathom how anyone could do such a thing. I told him I couldn't possibly know how to do his job, but at some point it had seemed important that I should at least have some knowledge of every subject matter on the off chance someone would ask me and that this preparation was warranted that day. It is not about being a jack-of-all-trades but about having a thirst for knowledge.

Warren Buffet and Bill Gates once were interviewed together and were asked if they could have one superpower what it would be. Their answer was to have the ability to have read every book there was. They credit their success to reading every day. Buffet spends close to eight hours reading every day, and while there were probably days he did not do this, the point is that he still did it more than most, and that's one reason why he is the richest man in the US.

I am going to make a bold statement now. I am never wrong when I give you an answer. Oh boy, what a narcissist I am, right? Wrong! You see, it is not that I am always right, but what I do is when I know the answer, I tell you; when I don't, I find it for you; and when there is no right answer, I express multiple viewpoints of which one may be right or at the very least the culmination will lead to the right answer for you that will be discovered once you weigh the options. I am reminded of a quote from Terrence Howard in the film *Get Rich or Die Trying* (not exactly where you would look for one, but here it is):

"I know I'm right because if I am right I'm right and if I'm wrong, I could have been right, so I'm right because I could have been wrong."

Next time you're faced with an argument, use this line; most people will get confused and then the disagreement is diffused and you can move on. By defusing the argument, that makes you right by default. Okay, so maybe that's not the best approach, but try it. It will be fun. Why I share this is because many times people just look for reasons to flaunt their ego, show you up, or simply just enjoy debate. It's very common in a bar, and having tools to defuse saves a lot of time. We know that time is a commodity you don't need to waste on these types. Many times a guy wearing a Yankees hat gets grief from someone who is just looking to argue to make himself feel better. There is no arguing the Yankees. They have the most titles, which is the ultimate trump card, period, but you cannot beat someone whose goal is to argue because the debate is moot; he has already won by baiting you into his world, and your reaction was his goal. This is how fights start, and when it's fueled with alcohol, inhibitions are lowered, egos become inflated, and testosterone starts pumping, and for what? Because some idiot can't count World Series rings. Move on, be the better man, and save the bartender the grief of having to step in.

Education, exposure to learning opportunities, and now past and current careers are what shape the credibility of the bartender. Most of us have experience in other lines of work. Teachers across the country are underpaid, and many work part-time behind the bar to make ends meet, as do others who have day jobs. We have touched on the actor, which I know a lot about due to my own experience and the plethora of those who reside in LA. I can only speak to my own experience in this facet. I've shared with you my past as a sportscaster and actor, but there's more. When I first came to LA, ironically, I befriended a rocket scientist (maybe I missed my calling). Ted worked for Boeing at the time that we met through mutual friends. He was older, but once he found out that I was a bartender he looked back on his past profession that helped him achieve his dream profession. He was the actual stereotype, working his way through school behind the bar. His course load was a bit more challenging than your average bartender, but I don't have to tell you, we tend to be a pretty intellectual breed. There was one skill that he had, which most bartenders do not, aside from a few gags here and there. He was a bartending magician, and he took me under his wing and mentored me in the art of magic.

I fell in love with the craft and could see right away how being able to use the bar as my stage would help beef up my tips, keep my patrons there longer, and even help me with my acting. I studied under him and by myself every night to the point that I became confident enough to even consider a career as a magician. Magic helped me land more auditions and gigs, padded my pockets, and even helped me with girls. I flew to Las Vegas to study under the great Penn and Teller. Teller was a friend of Ted's, and we met one night after his show and had a wonderful conversation. It only took one meeting with him to help guide my path. He told me the reality of being a magician, and while I was comfortable with a deck of cards doing close up, it would most likely be a losing proposition unless I moved to the big stage. I wasn't a fan of leather pants and living in Las Vegas performing the same show over and over again. Even IF I was one of the very lucky ones to get to that stage, I knew it wasn't for me. It was not a disappointing revelation but another valuable lesson and experience.

My magic would entertain my patrons for years to come without a dream of grandeur, and that was okay for me. When people come to the bar now, I am known as the bartender who does magic, and my tricks are quick hitting and powerful. I have crafted my short sets to make an impact but not consume my time and keep me from my job. I continued to use magic as a tool for the bar and my acting. As for being an actor, everyone seems to have an interest in the stories I have to share. Who have you worked with? What have you acted in? Have you ever done a love scene? Is the casting couch a real thing? You get the point. To sum up my acting career, all I can say is that I did it for a few years starring in some of the worst horror films you could ever imagine. My mom was so proud to see my brains splattered on the screen time and again. I played a magician in a movie, which was fitting, and even played Ringo Star in a student film despite being six inches taller than the rest of the cast. I shot the entire film kneeling on apple boxes, which tells you the quality of the productions I was blessed with. I had a blast doing them, but once again I was not sold on this industry. I never went in wanting to do it for the art, just the money. I have no issue admitting that, and maybe that's why nothing substantial ever came to be—but all this has led me to my true calling.

A bartender's word of advice—"Approach life as an investor. Return on investment and opportunity costs should consume your every decision. Whenever you buy something or spend time doing something ask yourself at what cost will this opportunity produce and will my investment return something positive or negative?"

CHAPTER FIVE

It's Not Gambling if You Know You're Going to Win

I have met nearly every walk of life in the time I have worked behind the bar, and they all have questions. I have never had someone directly ask me to be a mentor, but I remember this one kid, Joe, who was about 25 and worked as a safety inspector at a factory. He did everything "right." He went to school and earned a degree in the area that had the highest job placement and earning potential for graduates. He was a hard worker, logging no less than 50 hours a week when he sat down at my bar.

He told me of his path, but I had a good read on him and asked a simple question: "What do you want to be?"

Befuddled, he chuckled and said, "Not this!"

"So why are you working so hard to be something you don't want to be?" I asked.

He thought for a moment and said, "No one has ever put it that way before."

I told him my schedule. Every week he would come in on my shifts, and the lessons began.

At this point in my career, I had been a professional poker player for five years. If you didn't see that coming, neither did I had you asked me five years prior. My bar magic had opened a door. My coworkers watched me perform time and again, and I always had a deck in my pocket. One day my manager told me about a home game they had every week and asked me to come play. I had never played, and when I sat down I realized I had been invited into a shark tank, as the years of experience from these new friends were decades more than I had been alive. I loved the game and the social aspect of making new friends, but I am a competitor and wanted to compete with skill rather than luck. I watched the film *Rounders*, and that epic line, "If you can't spot the sucker, you are the sucker" solidified my identity—I was the sucker. Faced with this reality, I began to study the game, playing constantly on Xbox and reading books. I was obsessed with beating my friends, and my hard work paid off as I began to crush the game. We held a contest with a point system to see who was best, and I came in second, one point shy of winning. It made sense because the guy who won had been playing for a long time, and while he wasn't the best, he was consistent. This gave me the confidence to venture into the casinos and really see what I was made of. I took some lumps, but it was about progress, and in that first year I progressed quickly and made enough to put a down payment on my first condo valued at over 300k. Becoming a pro took over my focus, and acting became nothing more than a hobby. Why wait for a casting director to dictate whether I would get paid or not when I could sit at a table and be the dictator of my life? The freedom was exactly what I had been looking for, and it complemented my bartending well.

When I started playing poker I was dating a girl named Amber, and we were living together. I loved her and wanted to marry her, but I was realizing my destiny and it was to win the World Series of Poker. This seems like an impossible dream, but here is what people do not understand. The WSOP is not merely the event shown on ESPN—that is the Main Event. There are over 60 events with lesser buy-ins but one ultimate prize, the bracelet and title of World Series champion. Amber never understood poker, much like the majority of people when I tell them I play. They look at it as gambling, but it is no different than being a stock broker. If you put in the time and effort you can be a winning player because it is a game like chess that rewards skill. While luck is indeed a factor, over time you can be a winner if you remain disciplined to your theories and strategy based on math and psychology. She wanted something more secure and had the misconception of most, that poker was gambling, and she did not want to gamble on her future. I loved her and made a compromise of sorts. I would apply to graduate school to become a psychologist like my father but would also compete for the first time at the WSOP as well. The decision of graduate school was not well thought out; it seemed like a good fit, but I would not put much effort into it and would rely on fate to dictate my ultimate decision.

I did not study more than 15 minutes for the GRE and scored over a 1000, which was good enough to get accepted. I was enrolled for the fall semester, but the WSOP was that summer. I prepared every moment I had and called my father a month before and invited him to come support me in Las Vegas. I would take care of his expenses, but his support meant everything to me. As I look back, it was unrealistic to basically have my life's direction rely on one tournament. As a pro I now know that many things happen in tournaments that are out of our control and can knock you out despite playing perfect poker. I didn't have this knowledge then and was all in from a life perspective. It was important to have my father there to see exactly what I had been doing and to gauge whether or not what I was doing was a flash in the pan, a gambling addiction I was unaware of, or my calling. When he arrived he had 80 bucks in his pocket and said he needed an ATM. I waved him off and directed him to the blackjack table. It was the only game he knew, but I told him to do what I do and listen to my direction. I had developed the skill of card counting believing it would help me in poker, but the two are apples and oranges. Both are based on probability, but blackjack is solely math while poker has the psychological element to help gain an even greater edge. As we sat down, I instructed him while I counted. His 80 turned into 500, and I boasted a 1200 dollar profit, which was almost enough to cover the 1500 buy in. He was amazed at the discipline I showed, never going on a feeling and sticking to a system. We never even found an ATM that trip, and the following day I would take my seat amongst the greatest players in the world.

I played a very tight game, very different then my style now, and it was working. Halfway through the 14 hour day, a player named Doc Sands sat down at my table. I didn't know who he was, but he was sponsored, and I knew he was the real deal. He tormented the table and was made of stone. There was no reading him, and in order to stay in the game I would have to pick my spots, which many times meant avoiding him at all costs. Like a boxer in the ring, you can dance around for 12 rounds with a champ but you will lose unless you go for a knockout. I seized my chance and baited him to call all in with his 99s versus my Kings. I knocked him out of the tournament, but it wasn't till later that I learned he was ranked as the number one online player in the world at the time. I advanced to the next day and had survived a field of over 2500 players. As I sat that night having a late dinner with my father, we spoke about what I had done against

Doc and making it through. He was proud, but we both knew this was not success, and he kept the praise to a minimum. One thing I want to tell you, never play with a guy named Doc, which was rule number one of three from Nelson Algren's book *A Walk on the Wild Side*. I'm glad I hadn't read it before because that moment I will cherish forever.

I barely slept that night, and when I woke up to start day two my nerves got the better of me, and I lost my breakfast before I even left the room. When I sat down at my new table, Andy Bloch, a top pro and one of the MIT kids the film *21* was based on, was seated across from me. This was it; if I thought the first day was hard, it was no comparison to day two. There were almost 350 players left with the top 270 making it into the money. Much like golf you don't have to win it all to get paid, as it scales down. Cashing would be an amazing achievement for my first time or any time in a poker player's career. As the field dwindled, the bubble loomed, and I would safely make it through to record my first cash. Day two was not as exciting, and I would finish 213th and earn over 3k. I had high hopes to win it all, but my game was not at that level. I quickly accepted this fact and rejoiced in my accomplishment. I was disappointed, but cashing out and leaving the casino with a wad of cash changed that as we went to a fancy dinner and dined on surf and turf like kings. Once we finished, my father and I sat digesting our meal and the day's events when he asked me what I was going to do.

"What do you mean?" I asked.

"Do you really think you should go to graduate school? It's your decision, but I saw something in you these last two days. You played with the best in the world and beat out over 90 percent of them.

You outplayed the number one player in the world and one thing I saw, you never gambled even at the blackjack table. You had a system that you stuck with, and you were successful. If you go to grad school it will be hard and time consuming; something will suffer, be it your poker or relationship, but something will have to be sacrificed."

I've always felt that no matter what was in front of me I could handle it and be successful. I believed that I could juggle the load, but did I want to? Being a psychologist like my father wasn't my dream, and when I truly reflected on why I had entertained this possibility, I realized that it was to appease my girlfriend and cushion her insecurities. This was not a good reason, but I did not make an immediate decision. I had a few months to weigh my options, and I did just that. The last thing my father told me that night as we settled back in the room was revealing:

"You know when I was leaving, your mother wanted me to make sure you didn't have a gambling problem and were fooling yourself. We figured maybe you had just had a hot streak when you saved enough for the condo and that this was all a mirage. We were a little worried. You are not ready to win just yet, but I can see the passion in your game and how disciplined you are, never wavering or solely relying on feeling. There is a method that you go through in your decisions, and I think this is the path you need to explore. School will always be there, but you love what you do, and you shouldn't let Amber or anyone else stand in your way of truly seeing how good you really can be."

Parental support is so important, and for some they do not have it. That is okay if you can dig down deep and believe in yourself. I didn't need the support because I believed. It sure was a lift to know that my parents were right behind me and believed in me. I had shown them that it's not gambling if you know you will win in the long run, and that is a gift that far outweighed beating Doc or collecting my winnings. Over the next few months, I faced my impending future much like a poker decision, weighing the odds and doing the math. I figured that it would take five years before I could work full time as a psychologist, and that was not guaranteed. I would be five years older and six figures in debt while hopefully earning an income of 80k a year. For five years I would have to truly be all in, and poker would suffer because I wouldn't have the time to play while focusing on my studies. At that point I had more money in my account and zero debt aside from a mortgage, which was comparable to rent anyways. Then came the math that was most telling. If I made 80k I could expect to take home 50k working full-time; however, with student loans I would have to pay close to $1000 every month. Really I would be taking home closer to 40k. This was discouraging, especially for a career I wasn't really passionate about. I was taking home 50k a year working less than 30 hours a week at the bar with plenty of free time to travel and the ability to splurge on life's luxuries whenever or however frequently I desired. As for poker, even if I broke even, I would still be financially better off in five years, even if I didn't save a penny more, and at least I wouldn't owe over 100k. When it comes to investing, many people think that it means stocks, real estate, or savings, but if you look at it the way I do, by not spending or having debt with interest, you are still investing. The glaring truth was that I would never become independently wealthy in this field, although it did offer comfort and sounded good at dinner talks.

I managed to remain undecided even through orientation, and on the first day of class I had to make sure that my financial aid had gone through. As I waited in the office for my appointment, it all became clear: I don't want to be comfortable. I want to be happy. Sitting on your butt is comfortable, but if you do it long enough you will never be able to reach your true potential. As I walked into the office, I decided I didn't want to sit on my butt any longer—I wanted to stand. Rather than using the next five years studying a subject just to get by, I would enroll in poker grad school and see just how far I could really take this. Most people quit before the miracle happens, and what they don't realize is that if they had stayed after it for just a bit longer, they would have realized their dream. I knew deep down that if I walked away from poker without truly going for it, one day I would wake up filled with regret and probably even resentment toward Amber. I could blame her for how my life ended up, and while it may have ended up comfortably, I couldn't see myself living with that regret of not knowing.

The financial aid officer smiled as I walked in and said, "You're all set. When's your first class?"

I gave a chuckle and said, "About that, can I defer this semester? I don't think this is going to work for me."

Surprised, she nodded and did not try to talk me out of it. With no real further explanation she placed the deferment, and I was out the door. As I skipped across the courtyard of the campus, I was elated. I was going to go for it! This did not go over well with Amber, but she didn't put up much of a fight. We had many other problems, and later on it became apparent we were not a good match. It probably took longer than it should have, but we split ways a year later, and it was quite cordial.

As for Joe, I shared this story with him and must have inspired him. He began to open up, instantly telling me how he loved music and had once played in a band that opened for his favorite band. I had never heard of the band he mentioned, but I asked him, "If this is what gives you joy in life, why did you quit?"

Like so many before, he said his parents told him it was impractical and he needed to think about his future. I hate hearing about parents who were not like mine because they have so much influence over our lives. His parents were not at fault; they loved their son and like most wanted him to be safe and protected. I shared this notion with him, which he agreed with, but then I paused for a moment and began to open his eyes.

"Joe, your parents were right (he began to lower his eyes); they were right that you need to think about YOUR future. It is not their life. They have lived theirs, so it's not their future, it is yours. If you want to be a 99 percenter so you can go to sleep with acceptance then by all means, but I don't think you would be talking this way if you were. Life is too short to take the easier, softer way."

He shook his head and said, "Yes, you're right. I'm wasting my time."

I interrupted and said, "You're not wasting your time, you're just walking on someone else's path. Take this as a learning opportunity. You haven't wasted your time; it just took you longer to realize where you didn't want to be. Today is the youngest you will ever be so embrace it and get started."

I don't know why I took interest in him, but I knew that I had wanted someone to tell me what I was sharing with him when I was his age. I had to realize these concepts on my own through self-reflection and self-education. There are answers out there to all our questions, but finding them is challenging and takes effort. Effort is hard to come by because we crave comfort. He told me he just wanted to be happy and had not been happy since he graduated.

I told him," Look around, my man, you've made it! You live in an amazing city minutes from the beach, and you're independently paying your bills and being responsible. Now that you have a foundation, build upon it. Build your own house; don't move someone else's house on your lot."

I had learned this with my experience with Amber. Sometimes I stray from this ideology, but it comes back with vengeance because it is in my foundation.

Joe came back time and again, and we discussed potential opportunities and directions his life could go. He would always come up with a *but*, and I was there to attack it. I told him to quit his job, but not today, to set a jumping off point and bust his butt until that day. He needed to line up the things that were important to him but, most importantly, to be humble. He was worried about his student loans, which is a worthy concern, and a reason he couldn't quit. I told him how they worked: if he quit and was unemployed there were programs to defer his payments. If he took a lesser paying job, say as, oh I don't know, a bartender, his payments would be adjusted based on his pay, and he could manage. This would afford him more time to truly find his direction and passion. I told him he didn't need to be a bartender, but what I was telling him was that there are plenty of options and he needed to find them. I was there as a sounding board every step of the way, reminding him that I did not have all the answers or a magic pill, but I had suggestions that he could cultivate in order to make the best decision for himself. A few months passed by, and he came in with a big smile from ear to ear.

"I just quit my job. Thank you, Jason!"

"Whoa, you did what," I laughed.

"That's it. I'm done. I am tired of not living and being unhappy. I am ready to start living."

"That's a great attitude. I'm happy for you, but I have one thing to tell you: you're not going to be happy."

Shocked, he asked why, and I took a stoic but stern position.

"You're going to be happy today for a moment, but tomorrow you are going to be scared because that's what happiness really is, a moment. Happiness is found in the pursuit, just like it says in our constitution. It is the PURSUIT of happiness, not the state. Be happy tomorrow that you are pursuing, not that you are happy in the moment. It is going to be tough, and the road ahead is not clear; in fact, it may not look like a road at all. You are going to have to cut the brush away and blaze a trail. I'm happy for you because now you are living, and as long as your remember this moment, it will fuel you."

He stayed for a week before packing up and moving back to his hometown in Kansas. I haven't heard from him since, but it is not about the result it is about progress. I hope he continues to progress and doesn't forget the talks we had. I hope he is playing music or on his way to his next endeavor. Hope is powerful, just like Andy Dufresne said in *Shawshank Redemption*: "Hope is a good thing, maybe the best of things. And no good thing ever dies." Andy broke out of his prison and found freedom. I truly believe Joe did as well. In the film it ends with Andy and Red on the beach, and we do not know how things turned out years later. But it doesn't matter because that moment when we break out of our prison is the moment we will look back on when we are old and grey and relish. I challenge the notion of hope because it takes more than that to move forward. Hope is a starting point to develop faith. Having faith trumps hope because it will get you into action in order to pursue happiness. Those that simply hope without faith are waiting for happiness to magically appear. Andy had hope but his faith crafted a plan and his desire executed his pursuit. Start with hope, have faith, and then execute your desire; this is the magical formula, but it has to be solved. The answers are not delivered by the tooth fairy.

The all-knowing bartender seems to have all the answers. What's the score? Was there an earthquake? Where's the best sushi? What kind of drink does she drink? We know these answers, but many have questions regarding life, like Joe. I don't have those answers for everybody, nor should you rely on me to give them. What I do have is an insight into many of the angles. Our perspective in the bar is unmatched because we take different forms. We can be interactive or voyeuristic, we can be introspective or extrospective, and most importantly we can offer suggestions from multiple viewpoints because we have a vested interest in your well-being. The reason for this is that we have seen so many people's successes and failures. We file them away and share them with you. This is why you come to us, this is why you trust us with your deepest fears and secrets. Now that we are credible, we can go deeper into the psychology of the bar beginning with the managing and interacting of those we encounter and how we can learn from this approach.

A bartender's word of advice—"Formal education can earn you a living, self-education can earn you a fortune." - A quote from Jim Rohn

CHAPTER SIX

Managing Life as a Bar

I have worked as a bartender for over a decade, but for the last two years I have also been a bar manager. Prior to taking this position I had always been a head bartender, but I never had any real authority over my coworkers despite having to handle managerial situations many times. The last few years with this title have really shown me a great deal about myself and management in general. There are many books that I have read on management, and I suggest reading them for those who are interested. One key element I have found through my readings is that there is no formula that is exact. Therefore you must forge your own style, and the one I have developed has helped me learn so much about myself.

As a bartender you encounter customers and even coworkers who cause issues, but with no authority you really have no way of solving these issues. In regard to customers who take issue with my service, I used to have an easy out: I could say, "Would you like to speak to my manager?" There were times in which I did not use this method and tried to resolve any issues on my own. Sometimes they want to speak to the one in charge, and other times there is nothing you can do; you just can't fix stupid. I am not always right and I know that, but let's break some situations down.

Some customers are simply stupid and are not equipped with the tools to see all the angles. I work on tips, so why would I do anything to jeopardize my income; I wouldn't. There is never a time at which I am trying to screw over my customer or willingly making them feel "less than." Many times patrons have a few too many, and they argue that there is no way they had this much to drink and that I had added drinks to their bill. Here is the reality for those of you who have felt like the bartender has done this:

First, I am sober and you are drunk; mathematically, who is likely to be right in this situation? Now I know that many bartenders drink and even get drunk; however, most do not, and even those who choose to drink tend to still be more on point than the patron. I never have this issue because I have never had a drink behind the bar. I take my job seriously and feel that an accountant would, under no circumstance, be allowed to drink, nor should he be, so why should I feel any different for my chosen profession?

Second, if a bartender does make a mistake with your tab, it's almost always in your favor, and very seldom would you speak up about the matter. There have been times in which I was not sure if I had rung in a drink because I was busy. In this instance, I always side with the belief that it is better to eat it than to over ring, and I have done so in this type of situation.

Finally, there are times when I am wrong, and most of these times are easily discerned because it is not the drink that they were having. They notice a bourbon on their tab when all they had was vodka. I try to always be polite and take care of it immediately, explaining that I must have hit the button on accident—case closed, all parties are happy.

Now, as a manager, I am the last line of authority, which is nice at times, but when you open the door you let the good in with the bad. As we look at this previous example, some will not accept the situation and ask to speak to a manager. Well, sir, you are! This is not always the best place for me to be, and it usually is reflected by the tip, but I have a responsibility to the bar, first and foremost. This leads me to my favorite altercation, of the physical variety.

I have a doorman, but many times two guys full of bravado decide this is the best place, right here and now, to show the other guy just how tough he is. You may have found yourself in this type of situation, but here is the tool that I use to defuse the situation: I am 6'3, 180 lbs, and not really an imposing figure, so the last thing I want to do is catch a stray punch. When I see the altercation escalate to the tipping point of physicality, I jump in with a stern voice and say I don't want to hear it. Usually they are trying to argue their point, which is moot. I don't care who is right, because I am protecting the bar and themselves. I tell them I don't care who started it, but it's over now, and if you want to continue, then you can leave, right or wrong. This doesn't exactly solve the problem, but typically the idea of being thrown out of the bar and presented with the embarrassment of the moment is enough. When it is not enough, I tell them, look, tomorrow when you wake up, you won't care about this so don't do anything that will make something so insignificant escalate. I am not going to just kick you out, I'm going to call the cops and have them sort it out. When said in a stern voice with an eye piercing look, they know this is the last straw, and usually by this point my doorman is there ready to remove them if it goes any further. So what we can take away from this and apply to our lives is that we shouldn't sweat the small stuff. Why fight over the Yankee game? It doesn't matter. So he looked at you wrong, be a bigger man and walk away. Now, these are things that we have been taught time and again, but here is one lesson that you may have not heard: don't let people rent space in your head. That's what you are doing when you are on the verge of a physical altercation. You need to prove you're tough? Why, because some guy has an opinion of you? You have already lost the real fight within yourself because you have insecurities that you are allowing someone else to agitate. More importantly, your head space is valuable; don't let anyone set up shop and dictate your life.

I have never been in a bar fight because I adopted this mentality for myself when I was 14. It was the last time I was in a fight, and it was less the epic. It was actually with a friend of mine, Ty, in gym class. We wrestled on the ground and never landed a punch, but it was enough to send us both to the principal's office. The school I went to did not simply suspend you but called the cops, and we were both charged with affrays. We did not go to jail, but we realized in that moment that we were stupid and that the consequences far outweighed the reasons we had decided to prove ourselves. This was a bit of a scare tactic our school utilized, but our parents were not pleased, and we had to meet with a court counselor. The issue was resolved well before the meeting, but it was a lesson that we should always choose our battles. The law system is not always fair, but it is in place, and we have to abide by laws even if the penalty seems unjust. Ask yourself if going to jail over a bar argument is ever worth it, because that's what happens when cooler heads do not prevail. With my method I have been able to help avoid this, and I'm happy to say I have never had to call the cops. I used my mind to influence those incapable of doing so in the moment, to do so for themselves.

Working with other people is a challenge unto itself. I've read countless books on management, and if you want to learn from the best go straight to Peter Drucker and start with *Manage Oneself.* It's an amazing comprehensive book that is short and to the point. Management starts with managing yourself. If you cannot manage your focus, emotions, and purpose then you are not suited to be a manager no matter how deserving you may feel you are. What I mean by this is that in life we see people work in industries hoping to one day be good managers because they are good workers. This is a fallacy, and the two are not intertwined. I may be the best bartender in the world but making cocktails and change do not make me a great manager. For those of you who believe seniority as a worker entitles you to a management position, I hope for your sake and the company's sake that they do not make an error in hiring you. If you want to be a manager and a successful one, do your research, and then when the opportunity presents itself you will be ready. For years I was a head bartender and was not prepared to be a manager because I did not do the research. Fortunately for me, I had developed other skills unknowingly that I will pass along to you. These skills helped me with the learning curve until I was able to do the research in order to be the best that I could be.

Since I became a bar manager I have made almost every girl I have worked with cry. At my bar there are only two guys who work the bar, and we are both managers; the rest of the staff is composed of women with the exception of the kitchen and bar-backs/doormen. I am not proud of this record, but it was necessary, and some could even say, "Well, women are emotional and cry." I don't buy into this, but how I handled the situations were, at the time, to the best of my abilities. There are a few examples that stand out in which I had to confront my coworkers for poor performance, and all three involved drinking on the job. You know how I feel about this practice and the misconception that it is okay for them to partake. My owner actually wants the staff to take shots with customers because it usually boosts sales, so I can see his point. He is the owner, and what he says goes, but I am the manager, and I have to deal with this allowance to the best of my ability. It is certainly a challenge, but I tell my staff you can have drinks as long as the customer is buying them for you and themselves and hopefully the table. I don't know why customers feel the need to involve the staff, but I digress. I instruct them that I do not know their limits and they are adults so use their own judgment, and I will never say a word—UNLESS. This is the big point I stress: if you have too much you will get in trouble, especially if I notice it, and more so if it hinders your performance. The times when these girls cried, they all had had too much to drink. It is hard enough to deal with customers who drink, but employees is a different matter. If I don't handle it well, it will come back to me via the owner.

Mary was a 22-year old who was defiant and a bit of a hot mess. She had more than a few complaints, but one day in particular she had come to work drunk. She told me that she didn't feel good and was really tired prior to her shift, but it would not be until later that I found out she was simply drunk. Tables began to complain, which happens, and I usually give the benefit of the doubt to my staff. When a table says they have waited for 20 minutes, I secretly roll my eyes because it was likely five to ten, although I have been in their place and it does feel like 20. They want to exaggerate their complaint, which is not necessary, so typically I tell them I will speak to their server. I make it a point to do so in eyeshot, and I did this with Mary. I told her there were some complaints and that I simply needed her to tighten up and give them extra attention, no big deal. I was met with attitude, which was bewildering to me because we had had a decent relationship to this point. An hour went by, and another customer came up to me to complain, but this time was different. Julie was a manager at a local competitor and pulled me aside, saying that Mary had been very inattentive, and she felt that she was drunk and could smell it on her. I knew Julie would only complain to me if it was serious, and so I pulled Mary aside again, this time out of sight to stress the importance. I asked her if everything was okay, but she was agitated. I persisted and asked if she was drunk. She exploded on me and began cursing at me and telling me how shitty of a manager I was. In times like these, you don't have much time to weigh your moves, but I knew that losing my cool would not be beneficial. I spoke loudly but did not yell. I tried to explain to her that I didn't care what she thought and all that mattered was that she get through her shift with no more complaints and simply be honest with me. She constantly interrupted me with an immature attitude and left me no option. I told her she was done for the night and would be written up. It would be up to the owner to decide if she was employed going forward.

I left her in the backroom and worked on figuring out how we could manage to get through the night without her. After consulting the staff and determining we would be able to cover for her, I began to walk back to talk to her again. Before I took a few steps, Mary stormed from the back, gave me the finger, and through her tears told me to fuck off. Well, that went well, I said. It was later confirmed that she was indeed drunk and some drama ensued, but she was eventually fired. The hardest part about these situations is the idea of power trips. It was easy for her to think that I was on a power trip to condone her actions, but I was not. Sometimes you have to take certain lines for the greater good of the business even when it is hard. She was in the wrong and I was right, but in this battle no one won; we both lost because of poor communication. I admittedly became frustrated in the situation, but I feel that even the most zen-like manager would have had to take the same course of action. This was the worst example of the three, but the lesson I discovered is that there is sometimes an imperative action as a manager and also in life that you must take in order to be successful and to simply be the bigger person.

Make amends! I can justify why there was no need for me to apologize and many would agree, but just like the bar fights that occur, this is why it is important. After the dust has settled, you approach them and you do NOT apologize. You simply say I was wrong in my actions and I could have handled it better. How you were wrong takes reflection: was there a better way I could have handled it? Absolutely, but maybe I was incapable of doing so, which is always possible. What this action of amends will do is restore the relationship and make you a better person. You have not given them control or even a sense of being right because that's not what you said. You simply have stated that you are not perfect, you realize that, and you will do better next time. This is more important for you than the other because many times as a manager when you go home, it will eat at you. It makes you uncomfortable and the outcome was not what you wanted, as it was for me that day. You may even have resentment toward them for putting you in this situation and mind frame. By making amends you have cleared your side of the street, and oddly enough the relationship becomes stronger going forward, and you can sleep at night. Unfortunately, Mary had to be terminated, but when I see her now, there are no hard feelings, and my hope is that she realizes she made a mistake and has learned from it. Being a good manager is not about perfection but progress. If we make progress, grow, and then learn from these situations, we will be better for it.

Most people in life want to avoid confrontation, but there are times when we cannot. I want to be friends with everyone I work with and encounter in life, but in certain situations, especially as a manager, you have to be wary that your kindness is not abused. I tell my staff that they are trained and good at what they do. I should never have to boss them around or scold them, but when the time comes, I am doing it for their own good, and it will be constructive. At no time am I wielding my power or on a power trip. I let them know that I don't care how they do their job. As long as I don't have to hear complaints, I will let them manage themselves. This is a key idea in life.

Micromanaging is detrimental and should be avoided in all areas, even with your relationships outside of work. Trust that people know what they are doing and how to do it, but make clear that when they don't know or make mistakes, you will help them to overcome them. I tell my staff that I will only write them up if they leave me no choice. I even say in the heat of a dispute, "Your actions are going to force me to write you up unless we can talk this out and come to a resolution; only then can we move on." I did this with Mary, and she did not want to take the easier way because of her ego.

Check that shit at the door, I say, because your ego is what holds you back. Being humble is a hard trait for people to adopt, but I push my staff to do so and this has been a good approach to having a successful workplace. It has been a while since I have had to deal with coworkers in this fashion, and I feel it is my method of providing a clear objective and understanding to my style of management and how I see the daily operations should run. Listening is the key to management, and if I am a good listener I can understand the best approach to each individual so that I am able to transmit my vision more effectively.

Managing your life as a bar may raise some questions. So how does this work exactly? These examples of how I handled these situations and learned from them are applicable in life. Listen to people rather than wait for your turn to speak. I learned this as a reporter. When interviewing a player or coach, many reporters only thought about their next question rather than listening to the answers. Many sports interviews are robotic, but if you ask the right questions you can begin to find your golden nugget. I was in a press conference with Lou Holtz, the head coach of the University of South Carolina at the time, when a question came up that revealed an iceberg. It was the last game of the season, and he said that he was tired and that this season had taken a toll on him. The next question was pointlessly asked by a print journalist who was simply trying to show how much he knew about the game. The question focused on the offensive line and stats. I couldn't believe that he didn't follow up on this gem that was ready to be unearthed.

As Holtz was finishing his dribble to satisfy the question, a colleague of mine whom I admired jumped in without being called on and asked, "Coach, you say you are tired, does this mean you're tired of coaching and maybe questioning your future?"

Lou Holtz looked like a deer in the headlights and looked off for a moment before saying, "Yes. I don't know if I can keep this up. I may not be what this team needs anymore."

BOOM! He had struck gold and ran with the story. It wasn't about the game they had just lost, it was the fact that he was going to step down. Maybe someone else would have asked, but if no one had listened and didn't follow up, it would have been another day at the office. Coach held a press conference the following week and stepped down. Listening is more important than your objective. Have you had this happen in your relationships? Have you spoken to your significant other and heard distress in their voice but did not listen only for it to be revealed later when the magnitude had become too great? If only you had listened, you could have avoided the outcome that had now become unavoidable and that now led to an argument or even a break up. Treat everyone the same way you would like to be treated, be it your coworker, customer, or especially our loved ones. Give them the time, patience, and ear to listen to them. Being true to yourself is a foundation that must be kept.

There are times managing when I have to be true to my position and cannot just be a friend anymore. I have to make decisions time and again from cutting a guy off, removing them from the bar, and, with coworkers, disciplining them. Can you see how this is needed in life? You have a friend who is a taker. Every time you need his help he has a reason that he cannot be there but when he needs you, it's unacceptable if you don't drop everything to be there. These are not the friends you need no matter how much "fun" they may be. You may find yourself in a relationship, and I have had my share, in which the one you are dating takes from you and gives little in return. It's called "tit for tat": relationships thrive when what is put in is received. Dr. David Buss discusses this in his writings, coming up with the concept of Welfare Trade-off Ratio (WTR) in which the weight one individual places on another's interests compared to their own can be characterized. Create your own mathematical formula for this so that you can decide if you are gaining enough from this relationship to warrant how much you are putting in. I tell people in their relationships to look at it from an investor's point of view and calculate the ROI, or return on investment.

I am not immune to this; in fact, I dated a girl who was a taker. There were moments that she was not and gave me hope that she would be a good investment and we would have a future together.

Constantly I was asked to help her with her homework, take care of her when she was ill, and do as instructed. Many times I did not mind because being of service is a principle in my life, and I enjoy helping others. But there is a line that can be and was crossed in which your service is being abused, thus hurting your ROI. The WTR was imbalanced, and I had needs that were not being met. When I tried to express these desires they were met with neither understanding nor compromise but hostility and frustration. She would say, "This is who I am," which was merely an excuse. It may well have been who she was choosing to be in those moments, but there were times when it was not who she was at all. She had been, and was more than capable of being, loving and caring, but chose not be. In the end, I had to hold my line and walk away, which was the hardest thing I have had to do in quite some time. I wanted to marry her and have a family because the projection was that she would come around and the 20 percent person that I wanted her to be would increase. Time and again I was let down until finally the WTR showed me that my ROI was not worth it and that any true investor would walk away. Sometimes you must do this to stay true to yourself.

As it says in the *Art of War*, "Know yourself and know your enemy and you will always win, know yourself and do not know your enemy and you will win half the time, and lastly if you don't know yourself and do not know your enemy you will never win."

I stayed in the middle ground hoping that I would eventually know her well enough to be victorious but what had happened along the way was that I lost my line and no longer knew myself, thus victory would never materialize. At the root, we can look to the golden rule for how to proceed in all manners of interactions.

I have the tendency to be described as stoic, which can come off sometimes as being an asshole. I maintain that I can be stoic but the asshole part comes because I do not wear my emotions on my sleeve. It can be annoying when people at the bar ask why I do not smile or why I am always so serious. Well, how often do you smile when you are at work, especially when you are busy? I am serious because I take my job seriously, and I don't smile all the time because I am not a crazy person. Can you imagine if you walked into a garage and a mechanic was under the hood trying to finish a job on time and had a huge grin from start to finish? Even if he loved his job more than anyone in the world he would look insane, because when you are focused a smile usually doesn't materialize until you have finished a job well done. So am I making an excuse and I am really just an asshole? Maybe, but I find it hard to believe because I practice the golden rule, and the tit for tat philosophy.

Treat others like you would like to be treated, what a novel concept. It doesn't matter what denomination or lack thereof you adhere to, every one of them uses this ideology as their foundation. When I greet a customer I give a smile and welcome them. When the order is taken, it is business and I am a terminator. I am going to get that order completed as fast as possible. When I return it is with a smile and well wishes that they enjoy their orders. When it's time to drop off the check, again a smile and well wishes. This is the service I want and thus it is the service I provide. Certainly we all have had bad days and have experienced service from those who are going through bad days.   Check that shit at the door. The majority of the time I don't do it and no one should because you're a paying customer and deserve good service. We are all human, so we can't always practice this perfectly, but maybe we can come close to that level through progression. Now, if you come to me and despite my smile and welcome you are disrespectful and demanding, you have broken the universal rule, and now we have an issue. I understand that there are outlying issues that I may be unaware of, but if I give you respect, I expect the same level in return. The way I handle this depends on the situation based on what mind frame you present and my own outlying issues that I may bring to the table. If I am having a good day I will try to kill you with kindness, which is effective half the time. If I am having a bad day I will go tit for tat. I will mirror whatever you are transmitting, which seems childish but, alas, I have a secret weapon. That weapon is that when you least expect, I am going to turn you. I will be very sharp and direct in my interaction, but when the time comes to settle up, just before, I am going to flip the script.

I use this approach: "Hey, buddy, it's been a crazy night, and if I was short with you it was not my intention."

Boom, I've got them, and the tides have changed. Almost always they may have a notion that I am some asshole, but now I have made amends and cleared my side of the street. Many times they will recognize in themselves that they too had not been adequate in this interaction, and they apologize or accept it with a smile. Their frame has now changed. These customers now will return next time with a better attitude toward me, and I can become one of their favorite bartenders. We see again how powerful making amends can be, even when you were not wrong. As I mirrored them and made it awkward for a moment, they in turn mirrored me, and the golden rule prevails.

Everyone has heard of psychology, but many do not take the time to understand it, and do not even realize the power it possesses, even when it is being used on them. I use it daily to better understand others and myself. Understanding psychology and how the brain works has allowed me to realize what it takes to become a better version of myself. With this, I tap into a greater power that moves me forward in order to have a more productive life. Experiment every day and use this mindset as a way of life. If you want to lose weight, find a better job, be a better person, then look at these elements not as life decisions but as experiments. We have all made the New Year's resolution to lose weight, and it's the easiest example to understand this concept of experimenting in life. We fail because we believe that we have to do it for a whole year, and that's a daunting task, so we give up, usually within weeks. Instead, make short-term goals and run an experiment, then reflect and see if it works. In regards to dieting, I have those annoying genes where I don't need to work out or watch my diet and can be lean with little effort. It is actually hard for me to become overweight, and I have never been in my life.

I was doing some research when the idea of experimenting came to pass, and I thought to myself, "I've always wanted a six pack, but even in my youth I never could achieve that goal."

It wasn't a law of physics so it was not

something that was a fact but merely a law that I had created in my head. I saw that Lebron James had done a strict paleo diet, trimmed down, and transformed his already impressive body into a work of art after only 67 days. I thought, well, 67 days isn't forever and it would at least be a good practice in discipline. If I didn't get a six pack, at least I knew that this diet wasn't for everyone, especially me. So I set out to do it, and after two weeks I saw results. I incorporated a light workout of sit-ups and push-ups, starting with 20 and adding five each day. This small progression would be easy, and at the end I would reach 350. Had I started with 350 I would have failed, but when I saw results after two weeks, albeit minimal, I kept with it. By the end, the workout was easy, and my body looked completely different. I had my six pack, and ironically I felt better as well. The challenge to myself ended right before the holidays, and I went back to my old habits, but something had changed biologically within me. It was no longer a mental hurdle, and my body began to reject the old types of food and crave the paleo diet. After two weeks I returned to the diet with no goal but a preference. I still maintain this diet, although I have altered it because I no longer need to be strict and can indulge from time to time. Overall, my body requires me to maintain the paleo diet. I utilize the 80/20 rule now, and after this small experiment, my body has adopted it. It was well worth it.

I implore you to do the same in your life. Maybe you don't smile or have a bad attitude. Run an experiment in which you have to make yourself smile at 10 strangers every day for 30 days, and see if there is a change in your life. Maybe you don't feel comfortable approaching the opposite sex. Run an experiment in which you make yourself approach one person, even if they work at the bank counter, and simply strike up a conversation. After you have run your experiment, see what you have learned. If nothing comes of it, oh well, but more often than not, something will change. I prefer 67 days not because I magically came up with that number but because scientific research supports that this is the average number of days it takes to change your habits and reprogram you mind and body. This is a psychological tool that I recommend and use, but there is a greater problem in your life and management of your own "bar." That problem is change; it scares us not because we don't want to or see how it could be beneficial. We fear it because it requires us to become uncomfortable and can seem impossible.

I always find people coming to the bar saying they want to change this or that. I want to lose weight, be more social, get the better job, and I tell them just do it. They want to change and they are telling me they want to, but when confronted, they start defending themselves and making excuses. It is like saying that your teeth are rotting and then saying how you won't go to the dentist because it is not that bad. You and I both see them rotting, but you don't do anything about it because you fear the immediate pain and discomfort you will have to go through. In life you fear the effort of the contrary action and the pain or failure you might endure. Everyone tries to justify to me that change takes time or it doesn't happen overnight.

BULLSHIT!

Change happens in an instant, and it can be life altering if you let it. Here is a situation in which your life could change instantly: Hurricane Katrina.

My life changed unwillingly in an instant, and there was nothing I could do. I could not go back, and I couldn't reject it because that was the circumstance. That seems drastic, but what if you believed that every change you made that would require some pain to go through but you knew would be positive were like this? It can happen by shifting your perspective. Again I bring up experimenting—use this concept to start your experiment. Treat this change as if you have no choice for the next 67 days to change whatever. When you come out of it, then you can decide your direction, but adopting this instant-change mind frame, you can begin to smash the fear and grow. Now, most people ironically do not fear change because of negative outcomes but positive ones.

How crazy is that? It's true.

What if I do this 67 day diet and my body changes? It will be so much work to maintain. WRONG! It will actually be easier. The best way to lose weight is to never gain it. During the three months after I had done this diet I was not as strict with it, but guess what? The weight didn't come back, and the six pack remained. It is like rebuilding an engine in an old car. It is going to take a lot of hard work, some heavy lifting, and even some discomfort, but once you get it going you just have to do regular maintenance. You don't have to rebuild the engine every day, just monitor it and do preventive care.

It may seem like I have gone off on a few tangents to mirror managing a bar as it relates to your life, but you can now tie these examples of life together with some of the bar situations. Treat your life as if you were managing a bar. Work hard with a positive attitude. Treat others the way you would like to be treated. Know yourself, and hold your line, and finally, experiment. Everyone you face in life has their own dynamic, but you can create a tool box for each one so that when you are faced with a problem you will reach for the right tool. When you are faced with a need for change you will have the knowledge to experiment to achieve the right results for you.

As Charlie Munger says, "If all you have is a hammer, everything looks like a nail."

Cultivate yourself and add tools to your belt so that when you face a screw, you won't pound it with a hammer but instead reach for your screwdriver. This also speaks of patience because when you have to change tools you are using patience. Patience is also found in listening, which we know is one of the pillars to managing your bar and yourself. Build a solid foundation with strong pillars, and you will see that life is but a series of interactions that you can either learn from and grow, or discard and regress.

A bartender's word of advice—"If you work on yourself and develop the tools you are given others will take notice, and you will be better suited to serve the world and make it a better place. When you clear your side of the street you will be able to not only help others with their side but show them a blueprint to do so."

CHAPTER SEVEN

The Dating Scene

The bar is the cornerstone of the dating scene, and I have had a front row seat for all the miscues and successes. If you want to truly see your shortcomings and defects of character, then starting dating; and if you want to magnify them, enter a relationship. Dating is one of the hardest obstacles we face in life because it constantly questions our value and pokes at our insecurities. I have spent years studying the art of seduction and experienced many successes and failures in my own life. We are taught that we learn the most from our mistakes and we should try again.

When Edison was asked about his 1000 attempts at making the light bulb and if he ever was discouraged by his failures, he responded by saying, "I did not fail, I merely found 1000 ways how not to make a light bulb."

This is a key mindset we must adopt when we date, and when we do we will be successful. It is a numbers game that will make us look at all our rejections from a different perspective. They are not failures, they are experiments and learning lessons that we can build upon so that when we find the right mate we will be prepared to be the best mate we can be. Here is a secret that you need to know: you do not have to experience 1000 failures; you can learn from the failures of others. Simulation will be a valuable asset so that we don't waste our most valuable commodity, time.

Simulation does not mean a computer program running tests using complex algorithms. You can simulate by learning from others and thus cutting the learning curve drastically. So how do we do this? Well, here are a few tools.

First is reading. Pick up some books about dating in subjects ranging from seduction to persuasion to simply dating. I came to a point in my life in which I decided to read a few books on how to pick up women. I felt dirty and ashamed because I thought I had sunk to a new low. I am a good looking, intelligent man with plenty of value, so why would I need to read books to get girls? I removed these negative thoughts when I realized that every successful man on this earth has looked to a mentor or a coach. Do you think Michael Jordan would have become the greatest by coaching himself and not listening to Dean Smith or Phil Jackson? He was humble enough to tap into his greatest strength of humility. Socrates mentored Plato, who in turn mentored Aristotle. If these examples needed mentors then would it be safe to say that we can remove our pride enough to look for help in something as unimportant as dating? The books are the first step in creating a foundation so that we can better understand the opposite sex and the psychology of dating.

Second, there is active simulation. Once we are equipped with this knowledge base we can begin to utilize these tools and experiment on our own— what works for us and what does not—in order to cultivate our own method.

Finally, there is the cutting curve simulation. We simulate through others and their experiences, which we will begin to learn from in the coming pages. By learning from others' successes and failures, we can avoid making mistakes on our own and expedite our success by mirroring the successes of others.

As Picasso said, "Good artists copy and great artists steal."

You won't have to steal anything because it is free for the taking, and as you will see from my front row seat, I will help you understand many of the mistakes I see constantly and discover how to curtail them in order to create success for you.

I know there are women reading, and we will help you out as well, but we will start with the guys, since they are typically the first to make the approach. Guys, this is going to sting, but most of you have been sold a bag of beans, and sadly it is the women who have been the salespeople.

The first rule I am going to tell you is to STOP BUYING GIRLS DRINKS. This does not work at all, and yet everyone woman will tell you that if you want to talk to them, you should start out by doing so. They aren't trying to get over on you and score free drinks (although some may); rather, they think that this is a polite and kind gesture. It is, and 50 years ago it may very well have been the key to success, but we have all by now become savvy to this antic. A guy buys a drink, and subconsciously he is trying to buy the woman's time. This puts you at a disadvantage from the onset because you are not confident enough to rely on yourself to make an impression, and the "gift" of a drink actually lowers your status, unless the girl is already attracted to you. If this is the case, it is all the more reason not to buy a drink. Think of her as a queen; if you deliver gifts then you are a peasant to her, and you will have to spend the rest of whatever time she allows trying to raise your status. You can argue this if you would like, but know that you are activating a cognitive bias. The mis-weighing bias is that this is how it has been, and, without any real confirmation, you value it higher without truly weighing the validity of it. Certainly this approach can work, and I can also tell you that a broken clock is right at least twice a day. I don't recommend this approach ever; however, there is a positive status-raising opportunity to use when buying a drink.

After you have spent some time and feel a sense of mutual admiration, if your drink is empty and hers is at least halfway finished, then it is an acceptable move to offer to buy her a drink. This shows the kindness you were trying to lead with, but its value is higher now, and by doing so now your status will raise. It shows that you are not selfish but considerate. Do not be an idiot and try to buy her a drink when she has a full glass in front of her; she will not think anything of it, and it will make you look like you're not attentive to your surroundings. So now that I have stolen your go-to move, what should you do?

Be interesting!

It is that simple. A few years ago I did seminars when the pickup artist industry was booming. I had thoughts of making a career from it, but those were short lived as I found poker to be my career of choice. I simply wanted to test my knowledge and see if it could work for others. It was also an opportunity to learn more about the mistakes of others—again, simulation. Being interesting is easier said than done, and it will take some self-reflection. We make the constant error of leading with uninteresting information such as what we do, where we are from, where we went to school, and our favorite sports teams. What is worse is that we ask them these questions that they have heard a thousand times. Never talk sports unless she brings it up or is wearing a jersey. Even a T-shirt is a no go because that does not mean she is a fan but most likely is merely trying to fit in. Most believe that they are defined by their job and origin, but we are not. Many times it is not as interesting to most unless you were born in a foreign country or work as an astronaut. Whatever you do, never ask if they have been at the bar you are at before; if I hear this from behind the bar, I shake my head, chuckle, and wish I could give you a body bag right then and there.

"Jason, you're killing me. You're taking all my best moves," you might say. But don't worry, baby birds, I'll feed you. I am telling you what is not interesting so that I can prepare you to be an assassin with what is interesting.

The alpha male is the guy who was the star quarterback and started shaving and having muscles earlier than most of us. They are naturals based on natural selection. This means that they are merely born with the genes that give them a head start, but that doesn't mean they will win the race. We cannot all be naturals, but we certainly cannot be alpha without confidence. We need to stop listening to the naturals when it comes to women because they will inherently say to be yourself. It is true for them because of their genetic advantage, but once we have all caught up physically they will still have an advantage because their whole life they have experienced mostly success with little effort and thus have the confidence that has compounded. That is why they are the naturals, but we can level the playing field. In order to be interesting you're going to have to do some homework.

I want you to read books on a bunch of topics so that when the girl you approach brings up MAC, you won't talk about computers but makeup. When she says Vanity Fair you can tease her because you read the book not the magazine, but hold up, you have read that too. You should travel the world, but pick random places. This is a great subject because everyone loves to travel, and if they don't, they already know about the usual places like London or Paris. I went to Iceland for a week, and it was a great experience, but the value of the trip has produced great dividends in my approach to women. You mention it nonchalantly too.

If, for instance, she is talking about a museum she went to, then you counter with, "Oh I went to this great museum in Iceland that had this exhibit on whales."

You will see this catches her off guard but you continue for a few moments ignoring interests of Iceland and describe the exhibit as if it were nothing out of the ordinary.

Every woman I have done this to almost always stops me and says, "Wait, you went to Iceland? That's amazing. What made you go there?"

BOOM. She is interested. But, why did you go? Easy—you wanted to be interesting. But you responded, "Why not?"

Now you're adventurous, and she can see this. You're not afraid to do something extraordinary, and this builds attraction. I went by myself, which shocks women but says to her that this guy is confident, he doesn't need to rely on others to make decisions or guide his life. This is someone I am INTERESTED in learning more about. Do not make things up but be true to yourself, which may cause some discomfort. Go to museums, attend seminars, anything that most people only talk about, you are going to do, because when you bring this into your interaction you raise your status. Once you have done these things and the girl shows interest, you gain confidence. It is not a façade; it's your reality. And when you talk about it, you are confident because you are talking about something you know. When you are faced with topics you know little about, it is evident, and your lack of confidence is visible. If you try to learn as much as you can, then you will rarely be placed in this situation. You do not have to become an expert, but learn just enough to be knowledgeable.

The other day I was talking to a girl, and I asked her what she had been up to. She told me she was reading about black holes. Who in the world knows about black holes other than the fact that they are devoid of light and scary as hell? I DO! I had read Stephen Hawking's *A Brief History of Time*, and while I wasn't an expert, I mentioned it and added an element she was not prepared for. Like a true assassin you may come at me with anything, and I will always be able to counter because I have done my homework.

Those are a few examples I use to be interesting. The reality is that I have lived an interesting life to begin with, and you should see the reactions when I tell them I was a magician. I am always prepared to do a trick because that is inevitable if I divulge that information, should I choose to. Many of you do not have that luxury, and you believe you are defined by your desk job. You believe it is boring, and in some cases maybe it is, but this is not what defines you. Sometimes I am a sportscaster, a magician, simply a bartender, but every time I am interesting, and if you don't believe you are interesting, lie to yourself until you start believing it. I am a firm believer in fake it 'til you make it. Just like I mentioned about experimenting, if you are not interesting, you will be an uninteresting person, but if you believe you are, you can be. Whatever you are projecting is what you can be perceived as with the right amount of confidence.

As Confucius said, "The man who says he can and the man who says he can't are both usually correct."

The Approach

You have heard it before because it is set in stone: you must be confident. If you do not approach with good posture and confidence, you might as well stay where you are. In order to be successful at the approach I have some good examples; however, they are not guaranteed, and in some cases, no matter how well you are prepared and how solid you approach you will be rejected.

GET OVER IT!

Do not be crippled by the fear of rejection. Tell yourself that this was a good learning experience. Review where you could have been better and move on to the next. Once you abolish your fear of rejection and adopt the experiment mentality, every approach will be a success because you will either succeed with the girl or succeed in knowing that the girl was not for you and learn a lesson. We want to think that it is always something we could have done better, but the reality is that you may not be her type no matter what. You could have simply caught someone who was unapproachable because of something out of your control. Maybe she had a bad day, she's hung up on her ex, or possibly she's not even into guys. It doesn't matter the reason because of the resolve you are now going to adopt.

95

It was an experience that you will only take the positive from: I went up to her rather than going home wondering. I made her laugh. Maybe I even realized that she wasn't worth the time to begin with. Whatever the result, the take away will be positive. Remember that we are not in the results department but in the work division. We are putting in work, and when we hone our skills, the results will come, and the universe will open up.

I have found that a good approach is finding a good opportunity. We tend to look for the girl who is alone and sit down next to her. This can work, but the opportunities are limited, and we could miss our chance at an approach and go home wondering what could have been. Most women stick to the pack mentality and do not even go to the bathroom alone. Finding the solo act at the bar is rare, and so we will have to take advantage of other opportunities. Do not be afraid of groups and instead look for them. Large groups are intimidating, but you work up to that. Look for groups of three. Two girls together is okay, but you will have to win over the attention of both because if you don't, the other girl will fight for the attention of her friend. When there are three, the other two girls can talk to themselves and leave you to make your impression. There are many theories on what the pickup world calls "sets." A set is a group of women, and you must look to open these sets. When faced with multiple girls, this is to your advantage because you can utilize a social cognitive bias. When the group accepts you then the one you are seeking will be more interested because of the group's approval, thus raising your status. Look for good opportunities whereby they are in an area in which you can be heard and there is a sense of disinterest in their surroundings. Do not try to go for the girl in the middle of the dance floor. You are putting yourself at a disadvantage from the onset. You want to show how interesting you are and make it easier to gain their full attention so make it easier on yourself.

Deer hunters build deer stands not because they are lazy but because it is a tactical advantage. They place the stand where deer gather and are easier to attack. This does not mean you should post up in the corner but instead that you should look for positions that are advantageous. Try and do some research: ask your friends if they know your target, ask the waitress what she is drinking, and look at how she is presenting herself. Once you have this info you can cater your approach to make her feel comfortable and direct your conversations. If the girl is drinking a beer you can take a more casual approach, a martini means she is likely a professional or thinks of herself as "better than" (maybe both), and if it's a fruity drink, well, then you have your woman who isn't really into the party scene and just wants to have fun. This is not a hard truth but a good guideline to start from. Gather some information and then tailor your approach to this type, but be willingly to pivot should this information be inaccurate. Nothing in the dating process is an exact science, so being able to pivot will be your greatest asset.

Now it is time to approach, so I'll give you a few ideas to cultivate your own method. There are no one liners or approaches that will guarantee success, but that's okay; you will create an arsenal. One approach, called the "opinion opener," entails confronting the set and simply asking for their opinion on something. Online you can find a plethora of these to use, but they are generic, and while they have had success, I implore you to find your own and to use these only as a starting point. One I have developed personally is a destination opinion opener. I like to ask their opinion on where I should take my next vacation.

I will say, "Excuse me, but I was talking to my friends, and they were no help. You ladies look like you have done some traveling, and I was trying to decide where I should take my next vacation. I went to Iceland a few months ago, so I was looking for something a little different."

This approach has a few key elements psychologically: First, it says that I am interesting because I travel. Second, they look worldly, and I value their opinion over my friends and everyone else whom I could have asked, which gives them a sense of value. Finally, by nonchalantly mentioning Iceland I have now given a few options subconsciously that will allow me to continue the conversation longer once I get the answer. Interestingly, the Iceland aspect can actually change the roles, and now they are doing the approaching. I was trying to get them to talk to me, but now they want to know about Iceland, so they are wanting me to talk to them. This dynamic shift is the optimal objective to approaching. Flip the script so that now they are qualifying to you and trying to keep your attention. This creates an opportunity to use one of the greatest sales tactics of give-and-take, reward, and then wanting. Do not fool yourself; this is a sales pitch. You are trying to sell them on why they should talk to you and possibly date you. The most successful salesmen flip the script and have the buyer actually trying to sell them on being sold.

Once they are engaged, they are rewarded with a dopamine release because they are learning something new. This release creates a natural euphoria and the association of a feeling that you are now connected, but it doesn't last long, and that's when we create the wanting by taking it away from them. You give them something they like and are interested in, and then you take it away. As the conversation continues, you take control, and say, "Wait a minute, you never answered my question." They will be taken off guard and answer your question but inevitably they will want the reward again and seek more interesting elements you possess. To learn more about this system read Oren Klaff's *Pitch Anything*, and you can master the art of pitching, which we call "the approach." But what if they simply answer your question, and the secret weapon, Iceland in this case, doesn't work? No problem, we pivot.

They tell you about their recommendations, and that's your opportunity to explore and redirect. Your target says she once traveled to Rome when she was in school and loved it. You respond by creating a rapport by relating and making a connection to Rome. You could easily talk about the Coliseum and ask what she thought of it, but we have done our homework and are more interesting than that.

Instead, you connect by creating interest, saying, "Did you know that they used to flood the Coliseum and actually would reenact aquatic battles?"

Maybe she knew that, maybe she did not, but it shows that you know something interesting and thus makes you interesting. Once you find your point of connection, you know what comes next: we take it away. As she goes on about her experience, you say, "Rome isn't really my taste," and then you recommend something interesting and say, "Have you heard of the Maldives?" Most have not, and she may even be polite and humor you by saying she has. Then you explain that it has a glowing beach due to the algae and that it's an amazing spectacle and a place you have to see before you die. Again, we have shown insight, knowledge, and activated her dopamine because she is learning something new. The effect is heightened because of our give and take frame shifting technique. If you have experimented with different openers and found one that works, keep using it until it doesn't. Like a pitcher on a winning streak, you don't change your socks until you lose, so if it's not broken, don't fix it.

There are plenty of different openers, and the opinion opener seems to be the best foundation because it sparks a genuine conversation of interest. One reason I became fascinated with magic was because of a guy named Mystery, a pioneer in the PUA world and a magician. He spoke of little tricks he would do when picking up girls, and I thought, wow, that actually works? I started out using some of his tricks and developing a magic opener, but it wasn't until I found my own method that I found success. I had read about women's fascination with astrology and the universe and all of its "signs." I don't buy into this because I have done my homework, and there are 7 billion people on this earth, which means nearly 500 million people share my zodiac sign, and there is no way that a horoscope can encompass all of us. Even when we go a step further, the math says it is crap because there are approximately 16 million with my birthday, 666,000 born the same hour, and about 200 born at the same second. Are you like 200 other people? Maybe, but I think you can see that horoscopes are for suckers (sorry ladies); however, I have found a way to use this to my advantage. If this is something that they give some merit to, and it is because it's a multibillion dollar industry, then use it.

My approach is that I will walk up to my target and say this: "Let me ask you something. Has a guy ever walked up to you and said he felt a connection to you across the room?"

If they say yes, perfect, but if they say no, then you say, "Well, I'm not going to be the first, but..." And then you lead into your next lines:

"What if I were to tell you that I have a test to see if subconsciously the universe could make a connection we were both unaware of, and it would be fun to test it? Here's how. I have a deck of cards (As I pull them out, they usually laugh, but remain a little serious), and when I left the house tonight I wanted to test this theory, so I turned a card over inside this deck, and if you guess it then maybe the universe is trying to tell us something."

She is no longer thinking of the approach but more about the "game" or "test" we are about to perform. She chooses a card, and as I fan out the deck, BOOM, her card out of all 52 is the one upside down. I then stress that it could be luck but that 1 out of 52 is pretty damn lucky, so maybe we should listen to the universe. In turn, she will tend to listen to you. If she is with friends, she will invite them over, raising your status that is already on the rise, and explain what just happened. If this happens, then you shrug it off with little explanation as if you are equally amazed by what just happened as well. They will think it is a trick, but just shrug it off because you are already in, the ice is broken, and something amazing has happened. She no longer has her guard up because she is wondering what just happened, but something more important is occurring psychologically.

You have made her feel like a kid again, which is empowering. Everyone wants to feel like a kid again, and you have given her this gift. Kids do not have their guard up and are innocent, which is what you have given back to her with a simple trick. As a magician, I am not supposed to say how this trick is done but know that it is performed with a special deck should you try to adopt this approach. Be careful, though. I am a trained magician, so I know that my cover may be blown, sometimes intentionally, and that I will need a regular deck and may be asked to do another trick. This is fine, but don't become a dancing clown—humor them for one or two more, then, like we learned, take it away. I don't tell you this so that you rush to a magic shop and become a magician; I tell you this to show you that you can cultivate your own method for success. It took many months before I came up with mine, and it works very well for me, but what you need to take away from this example is more important.

You need to find your way of being interesting. That's on you, but if you can make a girl gain her innocence and feel like a kid again, you are giving her a gift that most cannot and even more never even consider. If being with you makes her feel like a kid then that association will be anchored in her subconscious, and when she thinks of you it will remind her of her fondest memories, mostly from her childhood. With this approach I also like to remind the girl that no matter how her night goes I am willing to bet that she is going to be telling her girlfriends for years to come about what just happened. This is a key element; you want the girl to think about you after you have departed. This builds attraction and makes your success for future progression more viable. Now that we have an idea of cultivating our approach through experiments we will look at the next step, which is the time constraint and "instadate."

Donuts and Swing Sets

You did it! You broke through all the fears of rejection, and she actually seems interested. So now what? Make sure that she is into you and that you are not coming from a place of ego. It is easier said than done, like all things in life, but there are a few cues that you can realize that will indicate which step to make. Obviously, getting her number is a sign of success, but the real success is that you made the approach in the first place. The number is the reward, but why settle for ice cream when you can get sprinkles on top and eat it before it melts?

A key step that you need to take throughout this approach and within the encounter is establishing a time constraint. Ideally you want to do this early so that you can revisit it, but the gravity of when is not as important as actually implementing this idea into your target. When you make your opener, you have hopefully mentioned that you were there with friends so you will eventually have to get back to them. Once you have established some form of connection, you say that you would love to continue talking but you need to get back to your friends and not be rude. This is when you ask for her number and then leave. You have created a wanting, and now you are going to take it away. When you ask for her number, she will have longing, waiting for you to call. In the law of averages, this is a solid move; however, for the more advanced, there is the "instadate."

Where I work there are a number of other bars within walking distance. They are all basically the same, but what you can do is postpone the number question and mention another bar.

I like to say, "Man, it's kinda loud in here. There is a cool spot around the corner where we could talk more."

This is called the instadate because you are changing locations and taking more control of the situation. Women are more progressive today; however, there are still thousands of generations that echo in her primal genetic makeup that subconsciously make her want the man to take control and be the man. If your target is up for it, great; take the lead, and go from there. This could lead to taking her home, but at the minimum securing the phone number and possibly even a kiss. This is the best case scenario. What if she is hesitant? Assure her it will be for one drink and you can come back. Whatever escalates at this point, you will have the upper hand. If you bring her back to her friends, you get the number, and you're good. But it could lead to spending the rest of the night with her, leaving her friends behind. If she doesn't go for the instadate, which is very possible no matter how sharp your game is, shrug it off, remind her you need to get back to your friends, and score the number. Now, there are plenty of different theories and crafty techniques to get a number or achieve the instadate.

Do some research and find your own way.

Like I always say, begin with the foundation others have laid if you're uncomfortable, and then create your own. I did not wake up one morning with these ideas and concepts; it came from reading and simulating through others. Make sure your ego is in check. You may want to do it your way, every step of the way, but show some humility. How has YOUR WAY worked to this point? Is it possible others have blazed a trail for you to follow that has a proven success rate? If you were going to start painting would you discard Monet because you can do it better? No way. That's a fools thinking, and while you may never paint like Monet or even want to paint like him, you can learn and take golden nuggets away in order to cultivate your own brush strokes.

I created my own instadate, which I merged with the idea of making them feel like a kid again. There is a 24-hour doughnut shop near my home with a small park that has a swing set right next to the beach. When I am moving from interest building to instadate pursuit, I paint a picture for them before I ask them. I ask the last time they had been on a swing and if they can remember if they had ever swung under the moonlight. In my experience, this is very creative, and it works on a psychological level, tapping into their childhood memories. What I have done is created a happy memory in which they unknowingly long to recreate. It is romantic with a tinge of craziness.

Who goes swinging in the middle of the night? I do!

That's why I am unlike any other guy she has ever met, and I challenge them to be adventurous and start now. When I have them on the hook but they are wiggling, I sweeten the deal and mention the donuts. I have created a picture that is nonthreatening and inviting. It has worked time and time again. This is not the rule, mind you, but merely a tool. I know that she may not go for it, and when she doesn't, I take the pleasure away, but in a transitioning method.

If she says no, I do not get bothered. I instead say, "Well, I probably should get back to my friends, so what is your number?" Or I transition it and say, "Oh, man, I can't believe how rude I have been to my friends. It was just so interesting talking to you. Tell you what, write down your number, and we can catch those swings soon."

This transition does not show my dismay or concern of rejection. Sure, my attempt was rejected and she knows that, but I show her it doesn't bother me by the transition. When a magician does not want you to see what he is really doing during his trick, he turns the focus away from it, and that's when the move is done. She is instantly moved back to that positive mind frame. Everything has, other than this blip, piqued her interest and now, once again, you take it away and mask the rejection by leaving. Most likely she will not even think about it. One thing to note is how you ask for the number: you don't.

You tell her to give you her number because asking can lead to a no. Tell her to write it down or input it on your phone. Psychologically this is a turn on and has a higher success rate because you are coming from a point of higher value. When you ask, it is comparable to that of permission, and you pass your power on to her. I know that this idea of power and control sound off putting, especially to women, but it is easier to grasp these concepts in the game of approach when we look at it from a new perspective. Most of us hate the "game" or "games," but it is still a game no matter how we want to discard this notion. Again, remember that we are looking at all the positives all the time. We can dwell on this one experiment of the instadate that didn't work out, but the reasons why do not matter because they were likely out of our control. She has to take her friends home, doesn't want to leave them, or, no matter how sharp we were, she has it ingrained in her head to say no. This is a two-way street, and while we have learned the give and take and framework shifting to elevate us, she still has a role in this and will be working her own frame and desires as well. Women are programmed to play hard to get; some make it easier to get, some can be moved off this position, and others are simply dedicated and hardwired to this notion. It doesn't matter to us now because we were successful in other areas, and what we take away that is beneficial is all that matters. The success that was most important was that we got off our ass, tried an experiment, and learned from it.

I showed you a framework to create your method and mindset to be successful in the bar dating scene, but where we learn the most is from our failures. Even when the results are positive, we could still be using bad habits that we overlook because we were successful. Just like a coach watching tape, we now shift our focus to what to avoid. Amazingly, I see the same guys making the same mistakes every night, only to blame the girl for their shortcomings in this arena. Imagine how silly it would be for a basketball player to blame someone else for missing a free throw. No one is guarding them, and it's just them and the basket. But what if someone yells or tries to distract them?

Isn't it the hecklers fault? NO, it is their fault because they weren't focused. Approaching is a free throw: even the best shooters in the world miss, and every time it is their fault, no one else's. The best in the world, after a miss, will double down and practice even harder or look to find what they did wrong and try not to mimic that going forward. Remember that a failed approach is not measured in phone numbers but in failing to implement the tools you have learned. Let's look at the tape.

We touched on the drink approach which in my opinion is the worst. I have seen it time and again and it gets ugly. The guy subconsciously thinks that he has done a good deed and should be rewarded with her time. This is called prostitution. I know that may come to a shock, especially for the women. I use this word because they are comparable. Sure, a prostitute sells sex for money, but when a woman accepts gifts in exchange for her time, that is in essence a similar practice. Be careful, ladies, because while no one will admit this is the practice at hand, when you put a price on your time I think you can see the similarities. Ironically, it seems to work because a girl will be nice and humor the John, but only for a moment, because she knows subconsciously that she has higher value and her time is more valuable than the price of a drink. To make matters worse, guys keep trying to feed the machine like they are playing slots. The truth is that while, yes, once in a while, you may hit a jackpot, the law of averages are consistent and you will be a loser overall. The guy clings on, and as soon as he starts losing their attention he buys more and more, and many girls just take advantage of the free drinks until a tipping point is met and they turn away or even get up and move away all together. From the onset, you are at a disadvantage and begin from a lower status.

Most that rely on this strategy have no tools to overcome this imbalance. If they did, they would never use this approach in the first place. Many times when I am in the approach I will even ask them to buy me a drink. This raises my status and tells them on a subconscious level that my time is valuable. Many may read this and say I am a jerk, but if you do it in a humorous manner, it will go over well and, hell, they may even buy you the drink. That is when you know you have them. What if I am being a jerk by doing this? How many times have you seen "jerks" leave the bar with the girl and you ask yourself why? Jerks are confident, that's why. And while we think their confidence factor overrides this, they have probably used a tool that you were unaware of. They do jerky things, but overall they are displaying just enough positives on the whole to interest the girl.

No matter what opener, good or bad, you have used, this is just the kickoff to the game. Most guys have no game plan and rely on résumé. I've done this, I work here, I am an amazing person: LIKE ME! Let her decide if you are amazing because if you have to tell someone how great you are, then most likely you are not. When you are showing insecurity and lack of confidence it is a big turn off. We have gone over how to be interesting, and that is what we will do from now on. Girls are perceptive; if you try to flash the great job you have or how much money you have, then you are trying to promote something that is probably not completely true. If you are telling them how much money you have and you don't have a Rolex they will notice. If you are constantly telling them how great your profession is, who are you trying to convince? The truth is that this practice is really you trying to convince yourself that you are worthy of them, and they can smell it a mile away. I know many wealthy individuals, and they never talk like this. They are nonchalant because they are not insecure. They know the prizes they possess and do not need to impress you to gain confidence because they already have it. This becomes apparent to the target in the way they conduct themselves. If your conversation looks like a résumé you need to reevaluate yourself.

Then we arrive to the nice guy. Being overly interested and constantly asking questions becomes an interrogation that no one wants to be a part of. Yes, asking questions shows interest, but you have to complement those questions rather than waiting to deploy the next question. LISTEN and respond with something interesting that you can add. The other issue with the nice guy is that he is not a threat. He doesn't make solid eye contact because he believes it will make the target uneasy. Make eye contact but don't stare. I don't stare into their eyes but rather their nose; this makes it easier while looking like you are maintaining eye contact. I will judiciously look straight into their eyes because I want them to be damn sure that I want something more than just conversation. They want to know that you are a lion and not a puppy. Puppies are cute, lions are exciting. Be the lion.

Time is another issue. Do not try and spend the entire night clinging on to them. You have to build a sense of want like we mentioned before with the time constraint. The longer you are in the pocket the more likely you are going to get sacked. You have to be willing to walk away and let them pursue you. Ask for their number, try the instadate, but be ready to move on. Once you leave them after building attraction it gives them the opportunity to come after you later. If she does, great, but if she does not, you have her number to reach her later, and something happens when you walk away. She will watch you and how you interact with your friends. This is an opportunity to raise your status because you will not look like some needy loser. She will see that you have things going on that are important in your life, and if she is interested she will have to compete for your time.

Subconsciously we all desire competition. The cat-and-string theory reveals this fact. A cat is interested as long as the string is dangling, but once the cat has caught the string he walks away. Keep dangling the string; do not give the prize away. This may all seem like a lot of work and maybe even overthinking, but what good is something that is not worth working hard for and does not require you to study in order for optimal success? Most lottery winners lose everything, it's true. They did not work hard for it, so when the moment came, they were not prepared and lost it all. If you do not prepare and put the time and effort in, then you may hit the jackpot one night when your target is actually interested in you, but because you have not prepared, you will screw it up and lose it.

The greatest gift of being a millionaire is that you should be able to give it all away. That is right, you can give it all away because you know how to get it, which is the true reward. Lottery winners do not know how to keep it because they do not know how to get it in the first place. Work for it and skip the scratcher; lottery winners don't hold on to success, but the skilled ones can do it over and over again.

One more thing, stop drinking so much. I can't count how many times a guy has crushed it, and is a lock to get a number, the instadate, and even the sleep over, but they get wasted. I want to ask, why are you going out? Is it to have fun and meet a girl or to get drunk? And be honest with yourself. If you want to get drunk then go for it, but most will never admit this. They say it is to have fun, but most guys go out when they are single to get girls. Getting girls is fun, so don't compromise it by drinking too much. It speaks volumes about your lack of control, red flags are raised, and now you have lost an opportunity, and for what? You go home wasted and wonder what the hell happened. Most of the time you blame the girl because you could not honestly evaluate what happened. Of course there are girls who will get sloppy right along with you, and you might go home with them, but this isn't the type of girl you really want. Maybe it is, and if that is the case, own it, but don't get pissed when a solid girl rejects you.

I am different. For me, if I want to go out and have fun with my friends, that's what I do. Honestly, I don't go to bars that often because it's loud and distracting. When I do it's usually somewhere that is having a slow night. I am honest with myself, and I want my friends' company. I want to talk to them, not strangers, so we go to dinner, coffee, anything that I can do that will allow us to enjoy each other's company undivided. When I want to go out and meet girls, I am on a mission, and you really need to experiment with this practice I am going to share with you.

I make a decision to go out and meet girls and

so I set goals. I am only going to talk to girls I really like and not try to justify others as good enough. If I have to do that they are not. A goal will be to get a number no matter what. Once I have these goals, I am focused so that when I go out I do not get distracted by anything else. I will walk into a bar and before I buy a drink or take a seat I will review the prospects. If there isn't one that meets my criteria. I leave and find another place. I have gone to 10 bars in a night and in many of those places I never sat down or bought a drink. Fisherman who are serious go where the fish are; the guy who just sits on the dock waiting for the fish to come is usually disappointed and has to be satisfied with whatever happens. Take control of the situation and dictate your own outcome.

Many will say, "If it is meant to be, it will be." This is bullshit. If it's meant to be it is because I put myself in position time and again for it. That's what luck is, when preparation meets opportunity. You have read what I have given you, and you are prepared now to find opportunities. Don't just saddle up to the bar and talk to me while waiting; seize your destiny. We drink when we are out and tell ourselves it's because we are just being social, but are you really, especially when you are trying to pursue women? If you're honest with yourself, you are drinking for liquid courage. You must create real confidence, and others will see it and be attracted to it. Many times I go solo. This can seem creepy, a guy by himself at the bar, and guys who do this whom I see tend to be creepy. The ones who are creepy grow roots in the bar and look like a crow sitting on a fence. That is why I never post up or spend too long in one place that does not meet my objective. However, there are guys like me and you who are committed to ourselves and filled with confidence and do not need wingmen. In fact, wingmen are usually a detriment. They hold you back. The confidence is what separates us from the creepy.

I have two friends named Jack and Frank. Frank and I studied pick up and prepared while Jack believed he was a natural. He had gone to a small high school and equally small college. He was good looking and smart, but he was used to being a big fish in a small pond. Frank and I realized that we needed to humble ourselves and experiment with new ideas to be successful. It was this attitude that would lead us to the fish while not waiting on the dock like Jack. We went out one night with the sole purpose of meeting women, and we arrived at the W Hotel in Hollywood. It was a dream come true; the girls outnumbered the guys by a lot, and most looked amazing and successful. As we posted up, Jack wanted to get a round, which I allowed, but I informed him that our goal wasn't to drink, it was to pursue—but drinks made him more comfortable. As we had our drinks, we scanned the scene and picked our targets. Frank and I both agreed this group of 10 girls would be ideal, but Jack liked the bartender.

Dear Lord, guys, never go for the bartender; they are hired because they are attractive, and they make money off you by being cordial and inviting. Jack was unaware of this, like so many, and I challenged him to go get her number but to NOT BUY A DRINK from her. He was not up to the challenge and began to list a plethora of reasons why. He tried to reverse the challenge by saying if I were so good, then why didn't I make a move first and show him how it was done? I knew what he was doing. "You go first because I am too scared," was what he was thinking, and he was also trying to attack my confidence to make himself feel better.

Knowing this, I countered, and said, "You approach the bartender, and I'll approach the group of 10 by myself."

He would not go for it, so I did what any good teacher would do. I approached his target to show him how it was done. Five minutes later I came back with her number, and he was pissed. I told him my point was proven and that to make him feel better I would now approach the group of 10. I opened with an opinion opener that led me to status building with magic. I did a few tricks for the group and invited my friends over. Of course, out of all the girls, Jack latched on to my target and tried to compete. This is common because I have blazed the trail with the target, and he now can easily converse with her and interject on our conversations. I decided to feed Jack to the wolves and turned my attention to her friends, which created a wanting in her. Even more so, Jack was not prepared and lowered his status while unknowingly raising mine. Once he became quiet he left for the restroom, at which point I rewarded her with my attention again. Now she was more interested because the wanting had grown. I quickly got her number and Frank had gotten his, and so we said we needed to leave. We met Jack at the entrance and told him it was time to go. He was upset, but we told him he had had his chance; this is the way it goes when you follow the method.

As you can see, Frank and I were prepared and did our homework. Many times we have done this with success. We no longer brought Jack along when our intention was pursuit but only when we wanted his company and did not want to pursue women. Jack is a great friend, but in the art of war, which dating is, sometimes you have to sacrifice a pawn in your own chess game to win. Take these lessons and learn from them, but more so, use them to cultivate your own method and use them as a foundation.

Ladies Night

To be a true intellect you have to accept that you do not know everything and be able to see multiple viewpoints and possibilities. I always say that I am not wrong because I am constantly presenting multiple angles and rarely commit to one absolute truth. Now, I can say with absolute confidence what day I was born, and that is absolute. But when I say that eating well will lead to good health, can that be absolute? The shocking answer despite what we have been taught is NO because it is not absolute.

My friend was one of the best examples of pure health, running marathons with ease, monitoring his diet, and avoiding all the things that could jeopardize his health. He died of a heart attack suddenly one day, therefore proving that there are very few absolute truths. What we take from this is a new outlook to avoid thinking in absolute ideas and to be able to question things from different angles. In order to be an intellect, try and argue against yourself on every aspect you believe in. If you are certain that there is life after death, ask why you believe this and then learn why others do not share your idea. This is the concept we will explore as we address women. I promised to share with you some insight both for women and men. A woman reading to this point may say that this is for guys, but I urge you to listen to what I have told these men so that you can learn more about how dating is seen from the male point of view. For the men, the same is true as we dive in.

Women are seemingly the first whom we should look to in order to understand what they want in order to attract them. Sadly, this is not true, but it is not your fault, ladies. You are being honest but not in a way that is productive for you and potential mates. We all have heard that women want the smart, funny, nice guy, and this is true for relationships. It is seldom, however, that they are attracted to these guys in the beginning, which is why I have shared these previous concepts with the men. This is whom you think you want, but evolution is not on your side. The core of your desires commands your subconscious and dictates whom you select.

Ladies, you need to stop lying to men but more importantly be honest with yourself. If you really want the nice guys then stop devaluing them and knocking them down. When you give a number and the guy calls you the next day, you believe that this is a sign of desperation rather than believing, wow, this guy really likes me. I hate games and women say they hate games, but they are the ringmasters when it comes to games because of these types of neuroses. You are interested in a guy but when he is too nice to you or acts the way you actually want to be treated, you think that something must be wrong with him. Insecurity is a huge issue with women: if she is too strong, men will be threatened; if she is too interested, she will be taken advantage of; and if she is too easy, he will think poorly of her and abandon her at sunrise. These are valid fears, but rather than let them rule you, invert your thinking. Start looking at the men who made these fears true and what they all have in common. When you realize what this is, then avoid these men. When you see the things you really want in a mate, stay strong to those desires, and do not compromise.

Ladies, the next time a guy offers to buy you a drink and you have no interest in him say no politely, and do not let him rent your time. Nothing good will come of this, and the more you allow him to think that he has a chance, the more he will persist against your desires, and thus, you will end up having to do something you do not feel comfortable with. You are a good person, but the guy is not getting the hint, and despite your politeness you either have to move yourself from where you were seated just to get away or, worse, be rude to him. It is better to be up front and deny the drink. If he persists, be stern and say you are flattered but are not interested. It saves you time, and even if it is perceived as rude it is easier to move on then if you were to allow him to rent your time while falsely believing he has a chance and then be pissed when you are rude. This is how he will interpret it.

Women constantly feel like there are no good men left in this world, but look inward. There is one common denominator in the men you date and that is you. You are the one who selects them and allows them in. Some guys we have found are crafty, and it may seem that I have given these guys more ammo to take advantage of you. I have not; the guys who are seeking the information I have passed on are the nice guys, while the crafty slime balls have already created their methods and the ego and successes do not allow them to be humble enough to believe that there are better methods to learn from. The guys that take the time to put the work in are worth your time.

Do you not want to be with a guy that is willing to study and put work into something like dating? These guys do not just use this process simply to get laid or get a woman. They use it in every facet of their life, and what is beneficial for women is that they will use this method in their relationships as well. It is their work ethic that is their foundation. These are the guys you should hope to have a relationship with because when some kind of argument or conflict arises, they will be willing to listen to you and try any possible option to make it work out. I have had many relationships since adopting this approach strategy, and I continue to use the foundation of this work ethic concept for making my relationships better. I was dating a girl who had issues with intimacy. There were times at which I just wanted to be close to her and hold her, but she believed that this was just my way of trying to have sex with her, and she would pull away. Certainly this frustrated me, but I knew that there must be an issue within her I was unaware of because we loved each other. It was very difficult and took many attempts to peel back the layer of the onion, but one day I found the source of why she would do this.

It had NOTHING to do with me! I truly believed that to this point I was the love of her life and that she was the love of mine, but she did not know how to love. Even when I explained to her that I just wanted to be close to her and sex was not the reason, she had been programmed to believe this was impossible. I was battling decades of her life and a belief that was deeply rooted. Despite all that

I had learned along the way about psychology I could not reach her, and when there were moments of breakthrough I persisted and pushed her when I should have allowed her to go at her own pace. We broke up for reasons out of my control but also because I did not know any other way. I treated her the way I wanted to be treated rather than how she wanted to be treated. I tried to find out how I could love and show love in a way that would work for her, but the truth was that she had no idea of how to tell me because she didn't know for herself.

When we broke up, I wanted to find answers, and I researched like I would for anything. I really wanted to learn, just like when I was frustrated with approaching. I took the same mindset that led me to developing pickup skills, the same approach to learning magic and sports casting, and the same humility that said I did not have the answers. I knew that if I looked hard and long enough I could find them. I was successful and found many books on why she was the way she was and the same for me. I found through the book *Attached* that she could be classified as an avoidant personality, and I was at first a stable personality. However, through the course of this relationship, I slipped into the anxious personality. What I found is that as an anxious I would never succeed in reaching her and that the anxious push while those who are avoidant pull away. After reading and studying, I realized that I needed to get back to stable. Unfortunately, even reverting back to stable doesn't mean success because you have to be able to pull the avoidant up, and this is a difficult task. This girl was an unknowing master at pulling me back to anxious, and when I came back to her as a stable it was only a matter of time before I reverted back.

The reality of this situation was that she was an avoidant, and the reasons for this were so deep rooted that there was nothing I could do to pull her back because she needed to be willingly to accept her own reality and be willingly to change and work on it. This seems simple, but no matter how many people put the mirror in front of them, if their eyes are closed, they will not see it. They have to see it for themselves, and this is hard and uncomfortable. Most people do not want to go down this road because it reveals that who they are is not who they want to be. It is easier to just shrug your shoulders and say this is who I am, oh well. I am not this type of person, and I implore you to be like me. Say to yourself, yes I need some work, and no, I am not happy with myself and am willing to admit it and do the work to change. It breaks my heart that I could not show her how great she could be and help her to be the person she wanted to be. Understand something that she could not: I did NOT at any point want to change her to be something I envisioned but wanted her to be the person SHE envisioned.

As Marianne Williamson said, "Our deepest fear is not that we are inadequate. Our deepest fear is that we are powerful beyond measure."

I am not afraid of success and who I can and will become because I embrace the journey and struggle. After all, the reward is worth it. She is riddled with fear about who she really is and who she really could become. We all have our Hurricane Katrinas, and I tried to use this as an example, but it was too scary for her to move from being a victim to becoming a survivor. She grew up not knowing or seeing what true love looks like, and even when she was faced with me showing her the most love and care she has probably ever experienced, she had never learned to accept it nor believed that she even deserved it. Even as I write this, despite all the hardships I went through with her, I still love her more than anyone I have ever loved, and I pray for her every night just to be happy and find her way.

In the *Art of Loving*, Erich Fromm says, "To love means to commit oneself without guarantee, to give oneself completely in the hope that our love will produce love in the loved person."

I did this to the best of my ability, and maybe you have done this as well. You have to hold your own bottom line and know that every relationship you experience in life will end in failure except for the one you are currently in. In the same breath, all relationships in the human form will end once we die. If we can understand this then we are free to extract the marrow of love and enjoy it while it lasts.

My intention for explaining love seems like it may be misguided. Why spend so much time when the focus was meant to be on something as simple as dating opportunities at the bar? Life is not that simple, and when we do not think of the big picture we waste time, and it begins with the approach. If we are not thinking in these terms then we are wasting precious time with someone we need to try and convince ourselves may be worth it rather than find the ones who truly are. The section focused on men is just as important for women because if they are aware of these tactics then they can use them to their advantage. The next time a guy approaches you and seems to wing it, write them off. Spend time with the guy who has his shit together and has put the effort in. You deserve a guy that's willingly to be humble and work to get you. You deserve the guy who is preparing because he values you. Sure, it may seem like tactics are counterintuitive and that the man is trying to trick you, but look deeper at what I said.

I want these guys to better themselves and become interesting and enjoyable for what?

FOR YOU!

You are not the prize and neither is the guy. We act this way to attract others but the real prize is finding a relationship that is real and gives you everything you want. If you want to be happy then find someone who believes in the PURSUIT of happiness rather than the one who says over and over, I just want to be happy. This is a loser's mantra because they are ignorant. Happiness is not a state but a pursuit, and who better to pursue than the one who is willing to put the time and effort into the pursuit rather than waiting for the lottery to hit or the slot machine to go off? In order to do this, ladies, you're going to have to let your guard down. That doesn't mean to be naïve, but be willing to let someone in, and do not try to figure out what's wrong with them. Focus on what is right with them. It makes sense that women are always on guard and that's why we have to use these approaches. It is not to take advantage of you but to let us in. When the guard comes down and you let me in, then and only then can you make a true assessment of whether or not I am right for you, and vice versa.

In conclusion, I have given a few examples and tips for men and women to connect. Nothing that I have said is meant to be used in a diabolical way to take advantage of each other. It is only when we are willing that we will be humble and open to learn. When we arrive at this place a magical thing happens, and we transform into the people that we want to be.

Some may think, "Why should I do this? Shouldn't I be happy with who I am, and shouldn't the opposite sex like me for who I am?"

The answer is ABSOLUTELY, but do you know who you really are? Ask yourself this question every day and if there is any area you are not happy with, change it. I wake up every day and look in the mirror naked, and I look hard.

I ask myself, "Can I improve myself today mentally and physically?"

Since I am humble, the answer is always yes.

As Charlie Munger says, "Go to bed a little bit wiser than when you woke up." Then and only then will you make progress.

Life and dating can appear to be the size of an elephant at times, but there is only one way to eat an elephant: one bite at a time. The men and women reading this will wake up tomorrow with a new identity and perspective on life; there will be no more excuses, and every obstacle and challenge will no longer look like mountains—they will look like ant hills that we will step over, but it will only be one step at a time.

A bartender's word of advice—"You may believe you know what you want but until you know yourself you are merely guessing. Lead by example and work on yourself for others in hope that they will work on themselves for you."

CHAPTER EIGHT

The Cast of Characters

The bar is certainly the default arena when it comes to dating, but many people say that they go to the bar to be social. In fact, this is usually the cornerstone of every bar's business model. If they can attract customers based on an inviting social atmosphere they will find success. I can argue both sides of this by agreeing that it is indeed a social place. When bars first began to surface, I believe it may have been by chance. Think of the Wild West as a starting point for the history of the bar. This was more than just a watering hole, although it was just that. It was a place where travelers would come to rest their horses on their journey and briefly escape the worries of their hard lives and the journey they were on. We have seen the movies in which bar goers are playing poker and finding "love." Of course the love was typically in the form of prostitutes, and women who were not of this ilk were rarely seen. It was a social gathering and it has grown throughout the centuries to represent a place where you can go where everyone knows your name. Sound familiar?

The counterpoint is that many go to the bar and tell themselves that they want to be social, and they are nothing but. There is a bar that I know of in LA that opens at 6am sharp, and let's be honest, anyone waiting to get to the bar at this time in the morning is not really there because they are dying to be social but simply because they want to drink. Bars are successful in my opinion for two reasons: One, they cater to being social and creating an inviting atmosphere. Two, they cater to the drunks because drunks spend money, and that's the bottom line for any business.

So who are these characters that we find. There is not a bar that will openly admit that they want the drunks there as a refuge to foster alcoholism. In fact, it is quite the contrary, despite the reality of the bar in question. Even the drunk hangouts still attract normal drinkers and socialites and vice versa.

We will start with the fun ones, though, and those are the ones who go out to be social. These are the casual bar goers who tend to go out on the weekends or during happy hour. They are not really the most exciting from a research standpoint. That is not to say that they are not interesting people; in fact, I would say they are the most interesting because they are the ones who are doing something with their lives. Many times they go to the bar for the right reasons. They want to connect with their friends, coworkers, or make new friends. They tend to stay for happy hour and leave well before last call because their focus is not to get drunk but to honestly be social. They may not be aware of it, but they subconsciously can sense when the night is going from social to drunk time. For these casual bar goers it is the desire for socializing that is outweighed by the annoyances of others and their drunk behaviors. The socializing has now turned to annoyance because everything they are experiencing is shallow and no longer adding value to their evening. They have responsibilities that they prioritize. They know that when they go out Friday night, even though most think that's the time to go full blast, they cannot afford to be hungover because they have things to do on their day off. You can also spot these people because they will shockingly leave a half filled glass rather than crush it when it is time to go home. Shots are typically turned down because they are not interested in getting drunk. They are not interested because that takes away from their primary purpose of being there: to be social.

Now that we are done with the "boring" patrons, let's get to the ones whom we all know and love. The first is the "drunk girl—everyone's favorite! She is the one who is going to make damn sure you see her and who wants all the attention on her. She will jump on top of the bar, yell at the top of her lungs, and eventually be carried out (hopefully by her friends). You can't help but laugh at this girl; yet guys can't help but to put her on a pedestal, even though if there were a pedestal in the bar, she would be standing on it with a shot of Fireball. I like to call these girls "hot messes" because they want drama and attention and usually make a fool out of themselves. I would always advise guys to steer clear of these girls, but they are like sirens. Inevitably, guys will fulfill their needs of attention, feed them free drinks, and, if the guys are lucky, take them home so they can hold back their hair while these hot messes make a mess of their bathroom.

Of course this is a dangerous place for girls because they tend to black out and wake up the next morning trying to piece together the events of the previous night, hoping that something bad did not happen. One look at her phone log will usually tell the story. These are the girls who have mastered the walk of shame, but when all this is staring at them, they disregard it all and say they are all about having a good time. They are results oriented: as long as nothing bad happens, then who cares. When something bad happens, they play the role of the victim rather than looking inward and being honest with themselves about their actions and lack of control. There are people who take advantage of these girls, and in these circumstances the girls do become victims; however, had they not placed themselves in these situations they could have avoided the problem altogether. It is exciting, but there is a line they constantly cross that should be scary. With liquid courage, however, they do not worry in the moment, and fortunately the next day they can erase all those concerns by refueling.

I feel for these girls because they are fooling themselves, and it's obvious to everyone. They tend to be insecure, so they feel the need to attract attention even though it is typically bad attention and for all the wrong reasons. However, this need biologically is met, and there is no filter to decipher whether or not it was good or bad. It is like eating; you can satisfy your hunger with something healthy or with something crappy, like fast food. You know that eating McDonald's will not be good for you, but the end result you are seeking, to satisfy your hunger and be full, is met. Guys will be attracted to her, obviously for a number of reasons. She seems fun and is probably wild in bed. Well this may seem true, but the sex is usually sloppy, and she doesn't really enjoy it despite her antics. Her sexual antics are the same as her bar antics. They are a show to tell everyone—look at me, I am fun and having fun—but it's all a mirage. The other issue that is overlooked is, why is she doing this? It is apparent to me that she has a lot of baggage and that she is likely a therapist's dream. Guys will inevitably lie to themselves because they are drawn by attraction, which overrides judgment, especially when they too are indulging on the same level. As far as my interaction with these girls as their bartender, what a headache—they never know what to drink and take forever. They think they are entitled and everyone should bow to them, but my job is to make money and give good service, not stroke their egos. Thankfully guys will fall prey and order for them and pick up the tab. Lord knows, rummaging through the bottom of a purse looking for a debit card is like searching for the Holy Grail, and typically the tip is insulting if it is even legible. Beware of the drunk girl, my friends, and just sit back and enjoy the shit show because it goes off every night. Turn a deaf ear to the siren because it is a fool's game and a trap you do not want to fall into.

Do not worry, there is also the DRUNK GUY. You're not immune, fellas, and truth be told, you outnumber the girls by a mile. There are many different types of these guys, but the one who is comparable to the aforementioned drunk girl is the guy who needs to be the center of attention as well. He is the one who has to get everyone to take shots and make others drink as much as he is. He will always sing a hard rock song at karaoke, and if you hear Journey you can rest assured you have found your alpha drunk guy. I am reminded of a guy named Sam who is a great example. Sam is by all accounts a good guy on the surface: he has a good job, works hard (or so he says), and justifies how hard he parties by how hard he works. He always sings Journey.

When he first came to the bar, he had an infectious personality that others seemed to gravitate toward. I could see right through him and pegged him immediately. He was a high school football standout, graduated from college, and made good money. He had his game plan that I am sure has worked at every bar he has ever decided to make his spot: he bought everyone drinks, ran up huge tabs, and tipped great. I knew this was short lived and it would only be a matter of time before he screwed up. You may think I am being harsh and a skeptic, but I have enough experience to know that this was just an act. He was buying his friends right from the start and interjecting himself into this new social circle.

The "instant regular"—everyone loved him, and for all the wrong reasons, because he was the life of the party and got everyone drunk. They were using him, and he was using them with the lie of being social. He just wanted to be accepted, and with his trait of being an alpha male and childhood success he had a need for this social approval. He was not a natural, although he should have been. He is athletic, and on the surface looks like he has it all together like a natural, but this is a front. Some things did not go right for him, and as I got to know him, my initial perception was validated.

He was a single father and made no mention of the mother. I suspect that something tragic happened to her; maybe she died or was not a fit mother or wife. Very seldom does the man have custody unless this is the case with the mother. His son was 16 and actually got a job working for the bar. All of his new "friends" would say how great he was because he worked so hard and was a great father. Of course they did not know the whole story, and the reasons for their thinking highly of Sam were misguided and only based on what he projected to them. The general consensus is that if a man works hard and puts food on the table, inevitably that makes him a good father. We have a ton of social biases that are simply wrong. I like Sam, but for this purpose we are going to have to look at the real Sam, the one who is obvious to the bartender not blinded by a projected perception and seeing the bigger picture.

There was one night that was the defining point of what kind of man Sam was. He had been drinking all day with his new social circle late one Saturday night when his son, Rex, arrived. Rex is a great kid and smart. I knew that he loved his father, but there was resentment that was boiling in him. At his age he was not able to understand nor handle it, and hopefully it will not have lasting effects on him. If your teenage son has to come pick you up from the bar, it shows that you are not a "man" in my opinion, and it's pathetic.

When Rex arrived, he was unable to track down his father. No one knew where he was, and so we went outside. We heard a guy hooting and hollering from above, and when we looked up on top of the roof, there stood Sam. To the onlookers he was having his *Almost Famous* moment, and it would soon become famous for all the wrong reasons. I yelled at him to get down at once, and while laughing he began to walk to the side of the building to climb down. Great judgment always disappears when drinking, and for the drunk guy this is his finest trick. My bar has easy access in the back to climb up to the roof because it was built on a hill, but rather than going back the way he had come, he walked to the side of the building to show off some more. He lost his footing and fell over 10 feet, head first. His head was split open, and a pool of blood gathered where he lay. We ran over to help him. Ironically, because he was so drunk he did not do major harm other than the laceration.

His son drove him to urgent care, and Sam did not come around for a few weeks, but he did come back.

Lesson learned? Not even close. Now think about this seriously: does a good father ever put his son in this situation? I say no, and I lost a lot of respect for him that day. I had wanted to give him the benefit of the doubt in the hope that my initial judgment was false, but this incident proved I was unfortunately right. Most would not admit this openly and agree with my opinion, and so it became a humorous tale rather than a wakeup call. Many times Rex has come looking for his father, and this saddens me. The drunk guy constantly puts responsibilities, himself, and others in harm's way, both physically and mentally.

So why does Sam do this? He would never open up to me because, while I can seem like a therapist to many, the deeper issues are what drives him to be the way he is at the bar, and he needs a professional not a bartender. He buys the drinks for others and then forces others to drink like him because it validates the way he drinks so he can carry on. Misery loves company, and on the surface he seems like he loves life while deep down something is eating at him and he is self-medicating. The ones he aligns himself with make him feel better about himself because he is successful. Those who are insecure will try to surround themselves with lesser company to ease the fact that they feel "less than." I like Sam, and I hope one day he will see the damage he is seemingly unaware of and what he is doing to himself and more importantly to his son.

As for women, again, he sets a bad example because he tends to be a womanizer. He has a number of girlfriends who certainly have their own issues, but they cannot see past his facade. It is classic because he is the center of attention and financially shows security. These two components are ideal for the insecure woman, and both are actually using each other. He is just like the drunk girl, but she is more likely to damage herself while the guy is more likely to damage others. Again, be wary of these two types because what they present is usually a far cry from their actual character. I will say that should you choose to befriend them, be a true friend not a taker. They are surrounded by these types, and when the money is gone and the need for help is there, the drunk guy or girl finds themselves alone, which is a tragedy. They have good qualities, but they are overshadowed by these antics, so inquire, be real with them, and forge a connection outside the bar. They will benefit greatly, and you may find a true friend. But, like we addressed with the avoidant personality, always remember that you cannot save someone who does not want to be saved, and it is not your responsibility. I like Sam and hope he comes out well on the other end, for his sake and Rex's.

Now we move to the opposite side of the spectrum, the wallflower. These are the ones whom you will rarely hear from and may never even notice. To represent this character, I will tell you about Teddy. Everyone knows Teddy because he is a regular, and when asked about him, everyone says he seems like a nice guy. How can he be considered anything else, especially when most people tend to be polite when talking of others they do not know? Few people know if he is nice or not because he never really talks to anyone, even me! Teddy comes in three or four days per week on average and finds his seat at the bar. He watches the endless *Sportscenter* loop, drinking his Miller Lite bottle, and never uttering a word unless spoken to. In fact, when he wants a new beer he will place his bottle on the ledge and not even ask; he just expects it to be replaced, and Lord help you if it is not done expeditiously because then he will let you know, usually with only a noise and not even words.

Despite this annoyance, I never mind because he is low maintenance for me. Even when I try to engage him, the conversation is mundane and never worth my time. He doesn't seem to mind the lack of communication. SO WHY IS HE HERE?!?!? Honestly, I wonder this time and again. I think to myself about how much money he could save if he would just drink at home because in essence that's what he is doing, except his living room is the bar. After years of serving him, I began to realize the why. He comes in to be "social" even though he is nothing but. For him, if he is drinking in public he considers this to be a social action, but really it is a way for him to avoid reality. He is a lone wolf drinker. He may not want to be, but it is better for his own perception to be at the bar rather than the couch, because that is lame. Society supports this thought as well. If you told someone you stayed home drinking by yourself, they would instantly think that something is wrong with you, and I would agree. Drinking at home alone is certainly a red flag, but drinking at a bar, well now that sounds a lot better. There is no solution for Teddy, just a reality he chooses not to face. Knowing a little bit about him, I know that he has had some hardships in his life, and he does not want to nor know how to deal with them, so he drinks. It gives his life purpose, and, from a business standpoint, the bar loves him. They love him because he always has a big tab and is a consistent profit. We can justify that maybe it is the simple pleasures in life that matter, and if that is what it is and he is fine with it, then who are we to judge? I know deep down though that he is not happy but comfortable, and that is no way to live, at least for me. One day he may wake from his slumber, but until then he will sleepwalk through life and exemplify the wallflower.

The advanced form of the wallflower is the creeper. Ladies already know these guys all too well. Like Teddy, they come to the bar when they could save money drinking at home. These guys come out of their shells after the liquid courage has fueled them. Before this happens, though, they will find their place within the bar setting and stare. Often alone, they make others uncomfortable and lack social skills. They are described as awkward, and once the shell breaks they intrude on others. They break away from the wallflower title and move to creeper status. They hit on girls in an awkward fashion, again usually buying a drink for them. When their lack of game falls short, often quickly, they just sit next to their target and make others uneasy. Sometimes I even have to ask them to leave ladies alone, which makes me the bad guy, but I have a duty to ensure that everyone in the bar is having a good time and not being bothered if they choose not to be. I hate to do it, but it is necessary because with no women in a bar, business will suffer. There is not much I can do to help the creeper, so I must sacrifice them for the sake of the whole.

Now that we have seen the different poles of the characters, we find ourselves smack dab in the middle, and there we find the couples. Boy, can I tell so much about a relationship by serving couples. There are the good ones that, as a bartender, you see them but rarely hear more than an order from. They are having a night out to catch up and get out of the house. They have a meal and some drinks and head to the movies or retire for the night. Once I have established a connection, they allow me to converse, but I always keep my time to a limit because they do not need me to have a good time. It is a normal relationship we forge, and I love these customers because they are interesting and inviting. They love to share their lives with me about their new homes, recent vacations, or any issues they may have encountered. They ask my opinion, and I will even ask theirs. There is rarely any discomfort, and they are a pleasure to serve. Most couples are, actually, but then there are the other types that are very revealing.

They come in and spend most of their time on their phones or talking to anyone else except each other, and usually I am pulled in. They need me to be there so they do not have to talk to each other. They have lost interest in each other and thus rely on me to be interesting. In the good example it is a triangle interaction, but with these couples it is more like a V. I connect to each one of them, but they do not complete the triangle and connect with each other. When I have to leave them to do other duties, as soon as I am free, they pull me back in. Modern couples may not need me because of their smart phones. It's hilarious to me, a couple goes out to spend time with each other only to spend all their time connecting with others in a virtual space.

To each their own I suppose, but I don't want to be in that type of relationship. In fact, when I am dating a woman and she spends too much time on her phone, I get annoyed and let her know. It may not be a deal breaker, but there is a lack of respect, and everyone can see it. When I am with a date, my phone is silent, and I will often not even check if a message or call alerts me. As a society we have lost the value of respect and show very little when we pull out our phones. We can spend days on this topic, but you get the point. The idea of going out is to connect with others and our company typically, first and foremost.

There are all walks of life that come in and out of bars, but there are those who choose to frequent the same place over and over, and they are the regulars. The TV show *Cheers* was such a success because of its vastly different cast of characters. This is why people enjoy bars: they can find people who are like them while being entertained by a melting pot of others. The regulars are vital to a bar's success and a bartender's biggest thorn in his side. The bar loves them because it is consistent revenue, and when people are regularly in attendance, it attracts others to frequent the establishment. For most, if they walk into a bar that is empty they will turn around and walk right out.

The goal is to engage in a social environment, and if there is no one to be social, then the objective is not met; they move on until they find a bar that is conducive to satisfying this desire. This is why the regulars are key: they will come in no matter who is there, and when the newbies come in, they stay because there are other people there, even if they do not interact. It is the herd mentality, safety in numbers, and another cognitive bias that is being massaged to eclipse insecurity. For me, if I am hungry and I hear a place has good wings, I don't care if I am the only one there as long as the wings are good. That is satisfying my desire; it is no different. As for the regulars and who they are, well, let's just say they are eclectic.

My favorite regulars are those who are like the good couples. They come in to socialize, have a meal, and rarely stay till last call. They respect my work and show interest in me personally without being demanding. They come in once or twice a week and are a joy to wait on. However, they are outnumbered. Most regulars are demanding; they even refer to the bar as "Their Bar" and are constantly recommending improvements and lending their unwanted opinions and beliefs to anyone who will listen.

I call them "barstool prophets." They have a sense of entitlement because they are there every day. Their suggestions of operation must be right and implemented in their minds because they are the customer and are always right. My owner is friends with many of them, and he humors them while I bite my tongue and deflect. I suspect they do this to assign a sense of value to themselves, but honestly, I have been doing this job for 10 years and my owner for 30—just enjoy yourself and leave the business decisions to the professionals. It is amazing in bars how everyone thinks they know what should be done without any real experience other than being a customer.

The other fallacy is the belief that the employees are their friends. I would consider some of them indeed friends and have hung out with them on occasion outside the bar, but many are not my friends. It can be a little awkward at times, and I am reminded of a man named Lonny. He was a somewhat prominent figure in Los Angeles at the time and was more than a regular but a fixture at the bar and was getting wasted every day. This particular bar I worked at did not have a ton of traffic and was more of a restaurant, so there were many times when he was the only one there. I tried to keep busy, but it was inevitable that I would have to talk to him every shift. I worked there for years, and one day he came in with a colleague of his that oddly enough he was trying to impress to get a deal done. Lonny was old enough to be my father, and when he introduced me, he called me one of his closest friends. I was thrown off a bit at the revelation, and so was the guy he was trying to impress. I played the part briefly before returning to my tasks, but, wow, what an awkward moment. If you are trying to impress someone, especially in business, do not call the bartender a close friend. The image is never good for you because that tells him that you spend a lot of time here, and no one wants to do business with a drunk or what they could now perceive as a drunk. Regulars tend to believe this, and I am not there to crush them, but it can make for some awkward moments.

A guy like Sam came in with the sole purpose of becoming a regular. The first time I met him, he informed me at the end of the night he would be doing just that. Being in this business, I want regulars because they pay my bills and create security for how much I will make. I do enjoy the rapport I have with them and our relationships overall; however, lines are crossed time and again that make it difficult to consider them actual friends. The worst bars are tourist bars because of the inconsistency. At The Waterfront this was the case, and during the winter months I would have to be careful with my finances because there was never a given as to how much I would make. At local bars it doesn't really matter; sure there are slow times, but overall due to the location and regularity of customers, it is ideal. Regulars are the life blood of the bar industry no matter what kind of regulars they may be. I treat them better on average, but when they cross the line and make things uncomfortable, I will correct them. It is a type of friendship, but it will rarely exceed the interaction that takes place when I am clocked in. Many times I do not frequent the bar where I work for these reasons.

At the end of the day they are drinkers, and when drinkers drink they will take advantage of situations, making it imperative that I hold the line. Being a regular is not like the show *Cheers* and should not be a goal. As I have said, be interesting, not for the sake of girls but for yourself. A regular feels like he has purpose because he is unwilling to find his true purpose in life. Forge real relationships not contrived ones at a bar. You may find people who have commonalities, but the reason regulars gravitate toward each other is due to negative impulses. They want to drink, and they don't want to do it alone. They have fears and insecurities and find refuge at the bar because they are surrounded by others who share these feelings and do not want to confront them.

Use the bar for social reasons at its core, not to mask inner issues that you are afraid to confront. If you find yourself being any one of these negative bar goers, ask yourself why. I love bartending and look for the good in everyone I meet. I love what I do because it is social and financially rewarding. When I truly want to be social on my own time, I do not foster my fears and insecurities and am true to myself in what my desires are when I go out. I want you to do the same. It sounds counterintuitive for me to tell you this, but I care about the wellbeing of others, and I want you to be the best you that you can be. If it means that you do not become a regular but have a happier life, then pop in from time to time, and I will enjoy your visits more when I hear about your successes and triumphs.

Some of you may feel uncomfortable because of the brutally honest opinions I have shared. This is not an attack on any one individual, but a generalization. I can only base my opinions on what I see and believe, and if I am wrong, so be it. Honestly, I hope I am wrong about some of these clients I have shared my time behind the bar with. Actions speak very loudly, and it is only my perspective and experience that I share. There are regulars who have made lifelong friends at my bar, and that is great. All I am doing is challenging the reality you and others may have in order to become better and live a life that wakes you up every day and makes you want to tap dance with fulfillment.

A bartender's word of advice—"If you find yourself questioning your life's direction and purpose, remember the words of Marcus Aurelius: 'In everything you do ask yourself if death is a dreadful thing because it will deprive you of this.'"

CHAPTER NINE

The Multitasking Robot

Watch a good bartender work, and if you have never given this a thought, take a closer look next time. Once you have seen a really good bartender, especially during a rush, look inward and ask yourself, could I do that? I do not mean bartending per se, but how he works, focuses, and operates. The reason why many ask what bartenders do rather than accepting that this is just their job is that it seems like an easy job. After all, it does not take a college degree, which society uses as a benchmark for a more prestigious and better job. This ignorance is no fault of the patron because we make it look easy if we are good at it. I marvel when I think of a surgeon operating on a patient because it is a skill that I do not possess and also a skill I most likely will never possess. Tending bar seems on the surface to be an easy skill, and while it certainly is not as important as being a surgeon, our cognitive bias leads us to overlook what we are actually seeing. The skills a bartender possesses are not that different in their practice as that of a surgeon; only the gravity of the situation is different. If I screw up, no big deal, but if the surgeon does, well that's obvious. The bartender is a master at multitasking and has many things going on in his brain while performing his duties and is the surgeon of the bar.

Before we dive into what we can learn and mirror from a bartender's skill set, we must debunk a myth. There is no such thing as a good multitasker. So when someone says they are, do not believe them because science tells us that this is not plausible. They may be better at it then most, but studies show that a driver who is totally focused on the road without music or distraction is less likely to make a mistake than someone blasting music, texting, or quieting a screaming child. Being results oriented, the multitasking driver may arrive at their destination time and again unscathed, but in the law of averages they will have more accidents. You do not have to take my word for it, just do some research—it's all out there.

But wait, did I not just claim to be a master multitasker? I am not contradicting myself but rather telling you that if I had one task to perform I would do it more efficiently. However, I have a lot to handle and time is limited, so I have learned to multitask at a high level. The difference in what I do is a process fostered over years of experience. Muscle memory and habits create natural instincts, and thus my actions are no longer thoughts but instincts. It takes 10,000 hours to be deemed an expert at something, be it playing piano, accounting, or even bartending. I have logged my hours and can lay claim to being an expert at bartending. Some are better, some are worse, but I am virtually unstumpable when it comes to my work, something you should strive to be in your own area of interest. There are times when someone will ask me for a "Florida Red Snapper," and boom, ya got me. It is not that I was stumped, really, but that some other bartender 3000 miles away came up with his own concoction for which only he knows the recipe. Try something from the Boston Bartending Guide, and you will not get past me. Plus, I have a smart phone, and you will never know what I do not know because I can always reference it just in case in order to deliver the drink to you that you want (tricks of the trade of being an expert).

As for multitasking, when I am in flow, you will see me take multiple orders, ring them in while my other hand is pouring a beer, and organizing my next plan of action in mere seconds. Many times, patrons will tell me they have a big order, and I laugh and say go for it. Most times, even when I am not on top of my game, I don't miss much and can concurrently calculate the cost by the time I return their drinks without ever using a calculator or ringing the order in. This saves time, and it's hard for me to tell you how and why I am able to do this when most would be lost. A lot of bartenders aren't capable of this, but the good ones are. They know the menu and take pride in their work. Pride is a big thing; if you take pride in your work it will show, and you will be more efficient.

Raymond came into my bar one night and was a very well put-together man. He was super sharp and paid attention to details unlike anyone I had ever met. He had to because he was an executive producer in the television industry. When we first met it was a slow night, and I had the opportunity to engage with him. I remember he was hesitant to tell me what he did for a living, and now that I know, I understand why. As I mentioned briefly before, when most bartending actors catch wind that they are waiting on a producer, they cannot wait to tell them they are in the business and run down their resume. There are plenty of Hollywood stories in which this has led to a big break, but in most cases these customers just want to unwind like anyone else. This action annoys them, and neither party benefits.

When he finally told me, I did not press and instead brushed it off. We had our small talk, and then I became a little busier. I had told him about my poker career, which interested him, and as I became more occupied with my tasks, I continued our conversation. Amid this interaction I was taking orders, making drinks, washing glasses, and the whole time maintaining a connection to our conversation. As it slowed down again, Raymond smiled at me and said he wanted to ask me a question and hoped it would not offend me. Not exactly what I was accustomed to, but I said shoot.

"Do you have Asperger's?"

I laughed, not really knowing much about this disorder other than *Rain Man*, and said, "No, why do you ask?"

He said he had never seen someone do so many tasks at the same time so fluidly and precisely. He said that I never missed a beat and that every action I took was optimized. When I had to go to the other side of the bar I would always incorporate another task such as taking dirty glasses to that side of the bar or returning clean ones to the opposite side. What really impressed him was that despite everything going on, I never lost focus on our conversation and didn't seem to lose my

145

attention.

Laughing, I responded, "I don't know much about Asperger's, but if I was able to maintain a social interaction or even engage in one at all, wouldn't that contradict the disorder altogether?"

Impressed, he smiled and agreed, saying, "I guess you're just special."

"So my mother has been right all this time," I responded.

In this world many people are overwhelmed by having a lot of tasks that they must complete in a day and think that they are unable to do them all. It is not that they cannot perform like me behind the bar with multiple tasks under time constraints, it is that they do not take the time to think optimally. At all times in my life I am thinking, what is the most optimal way I can achieve all of my objectives in the fastest fashion? I never have a free hand behind the bar because there is something I can do with that free hand that will buy me a few seconds. Those seconds add up over the course of a shift and even a year and will allow me to accomplish more and thus make more money.

If you have a To Do list for the day, take a new approach and map it out. Figure out what needs to be done no matter what and do it first, but on your way to the first task think about what you can do to knock out something else. When you complete your top task where will you go next? For example, if I have to go to the DMV, pay my bills, pick up groceries, run to the bank, and make dinner plans, here is the actions I would take to optimize my time: Since the DMV is the top priority, I know that going early will reduce my wait time there, and making the earliest appointment available online will reduce it even greater. So I make the appointment, arrive early in order to cut down the time, and knock out my top goal. I've mapped this out, but on my drive to the DMV I have a cell phone and pay my bills over the phone or while I am in line. After that is done I know that the grocery store is the farthest distance, so I will go there first, then hit the bank, which is on my way back, and, boom—I am done. At some time during my drive time I call my friend and make plans.

Now, this is a small scale, but a simple notion of planning and integrating various activities gets them done. That's a skill I learned from bartending, and if you want to really figure out some big goals, read the book *The One Thing* by Gary Keller. It will change your way of thinking immensely and teach you how to break down a major goal into small tasks and goals that will be less overwhelming and psychologically push you toward your objectives and goals. If you want to make a million dollars, it will not just happen, and it will seem daunting until you optimize yourself and break it down. If that is your goal, begin by setting a goal of five years. That means you have to make 200k a year, which translates to $100 an hour. Once you have figured this out, 100 bucks isn't as intimidating psychologically. Now you can begin to figure out how you can find a path that will lead you to this type of hourly rate, and then you can begin to strategize. Maybe you need more education or a different job. Start educating yourself and looking for that job. It sounds like I am making it seem so easy and maybe you are saying if it were, then I would. But you're a bartender or whatever and will never make that kind of money.

Exactly, now you have to start breaking it down further, so you research and find that you want to be a lawyer. It takes about three years before you will pass the bar and begin working, and now you're in debt and only have two years for your goal. So restructure your plan and say, five years after I pass the bar I will be a millionaire. In order to this I will have to either work for a top firm or work for myself.—all possible situations, but that's years ahead. Now that you have your three-year goal, work backwards. First things first, you have to apply to law school and before that take the LSAT and before that study for the LSAT and before that find out when it is offered. Now this huge goal you have set has ONE THING to do that you can do today. Find out when the LSAT is offered. That is not hard to do is it? Of course not; a marathon is won by taking the first step but also by optimizing and breaking down the many tasks ahead, which makes it easier and allows you to build momentum. When you watch me work behind the bar, see that this example for the wannabe lawyer/millionaire is the same process. I break down my job by accomplishing small tasks through this overall process. The end result is that I make more money than those who do not adhere to this practice.

Why is this important to you? I am laying out a simple procedure to enrich your life, and unknowingly it enriched mine with Raymond in an unexpected way. After our first encounter, I left that night thinking he was a good guy and made my night more enjoyable. By the time I got home I no longer thought about him. He came in a few times after, and we enjoyed our conversations together, until one day he asked me about poker. He knew nothing about the game and admittedly hated the mere concept of gambling. Like usual, I explained to him that poker was not gambling and laid out why it was not in a convincing fashion.

He was intelligent enough to understand what I was doing and asked, "What if I gave you money to play with, could you make me money and we could split it?"

Most poker players drool over this notion because they are not risking their own money, and that is important to gamblers who are not true to poker. The true poker player is interested in this notion however because it could mean that they can play higher stakes that they normally wouldn't have the opportunity to play because they are actually risk averse and can play within their means. As a poker pro, I will never put more than 10 percent of my poker bankroll in play because the variance is too high. No matter how great a player you may be, it is simply good business. Some would take advantage of the sucker and be morally unfazed.

When posed with this notion I looked at him seriously and said that there were a few things that I wanted to make clear:

"Yes, it is an option, but I only do this under certain conditions. I will not play with your money if I can afford it myself."

I explained the reason I would make a deal with him is to put me in games that placed me in higher competition and thus higher pay days. I also explained variance and that since I was a tournament player, even the best could lose. I stressed that we could not do a one-shot deal because it would be unfair to him and that we would have to commit to a few tournaments. He was not hesitant but intrigued by this concept.

I asked him, "Before I say any more I need to know why you are interested because as you have told me you are not a gambler, and in this situation you will be gambling on me."

Taken aback for a second, he gathered his thoughts and said, "It's the way you bartend. Every step you take is with a purpose and calculated. Every calculation you make is instant and optimal. The way you talk about poker sounds like you are the same way when you play. I look for this in people whom I want to hire, and you have those qualities. You're intelligent and judicial. You make decisions without emotion, and I believe in supporting others who have dreams even if I do not understand them."

I said that was good enough for me. It was a great thing to hear, and we made a deal on paper that I would select a few tournaments and he would put the money up for those entries. If I lost we would get nothing, and if I won we would split it 50/50. Something amazing happened after we began our partnership, and I told him, "This was not common but I'm glad it worked out."

The first tournament I doubled our money;

the second tournament I doubled it again; the third was a bust but we were still ahead; and the fourth was magical. He had invested 300 for the first tournament, which was affordable for me, but I told him it would be our first test. He never had to invest again based on our success, and when the fourth event came around, playing with "house money," I told him the buy in was 250 but that it was a huge event boasting a field of over 5000 players. It was a bit of a crap shoot really, but the payday would be huge if we won. He jumped at it, and to be honest, I thought he was lighting his money on fire. I played some of the best poker I had ever played and finished 6th for a cool 26k. I had never seen that much cash in my life. The following day we met at a lounge, and I walked in with an envelope containing 13k and plopped it in his lap as he laughed.

The score was an amazing feeling, but what happened next felt even better. As I broke down what had happened in the event we shared some laughs and good moments, but then Raymond seemed overwhelmed with emotion. He did not shed a noticeable tear, but I inquired, sensing something was wrong. Raymond had produced a number of successful TV shows, but he shared with me that although they were reality shows, which carry a negative stigma, his were different. They were shows that helped people change their lives and overcome their hardships. I thought this was great but pushed forward asking why he was telling me this.

A few months prior to meeting me he had taken over a woman's abuse shelter and was remodeling it so that women could come there, get make overs to boost their confidence, and rejoin society. He would help with their confidence and with getting new jobs so that they could rise from the ashes of their misfortunes. He was raising money and that day was short of his goal with only one week left. He was well connected, but no one would help him even though all he needed was 10k. Now as we sat there, he had more than enough sitting in his lap, and he would use that to fulfill the financial requirement for something greater than poker or any monetary prize.

This was the greatest gift I have ever been a part of, and, at first, I only thought of how great it was for this guy to believe in me to help me work on my dream of poker. His gamble helped me, but more importantly it helped others whom I would never meet, and that was an amazing feeling. Now look at this story and use the concept that I outlined. If I were told before I started that I had to make 10k to give away so a friend could save a woman's shelter, at the time, it would seem almost impossible. It all started because I took pride in my work and someone took notice. Together we did something life changing for strangers. When you work hard and take pride in your work the results will come.

When you take the time to focus on optimizing and task completion through integration, something inside you will change. What starts as a process that you're unaccustomed to becomes a habit, and once that occurs, those habits become instinctive. Once they are instinctive, everything becomes so much easier. When I first stepped foot behind the bar it was overwhelming having to carry out all the tasks required of me, but over time and after adopting this outlined mindset, I have become instinctual. It is recognized and appreciated by those who choose to notice. When I came across the article about Lebron James and the 67-day diet he completed, which I mentioned earlier, I realized his humility. Here is a man who is arguably not only the best basketball player on Earth but also one of the greatest athletes as well, and he was humble enough to experiment with a new diet. The pictures were proof that it worked. He looked like an Adonis, and it made me think.

It encouraged me to try the diet, but at this time I was also doing a lot of self-learning and came across the notion of reading a book a day. Again, this was not something that I had ever done, but it seemed as though there was some merit to it. Like I have said, be willing to experiment because you can always go back to your old ways, but if there is a benefit, what do you really have to lose? You only have something to gain even if it is the knowledge that it did not work for you. I thought about doing a book a day and this diet with a small workout. Many times I was faced with doing something like a New Year's resolution, but like most of us a year was so long, and I failed many times. When I thought about 67 days, it seemed doable. But a book a day, a diet, a light workout, and all this with my already busy life, how could I do it? I began to think like I would behind the bar and map it out in an optimal way. No matter what, I would stick to the diet. As for the workout, it was simple and based on the scale or progression. And the reading, well, I would begin buying a bunch of books off a recommended book list I had found that purported to enrich one's life and simply get started.

The diet would be the easy part—buy a bunch of fruit to snack on, and I found that if I went to Whole Foods they would even cook my meals for me for two bucks, easy enough. I could also go to a dinner and order omelets, so this part of my 67-day challenge was taken care of. The workout wouldn't take much time, and I could do it while I played online poker, again integrating to save time. When I started, I found the hard part was finding time to read a whole book in a day, so I began to break that concept down. First, I realized that all books are not created equal, so my goal would be 100 to 200 pages, since some of my books were shorter while others were longer. I also researched speed reading, but what I found was even better. There are negative ideas about speed reading, but what I realized was that for many books you do not actually have to read every page. Books are typically 20 percent useful and 80 percent fluff. I wasn't reading many novels although I had some classic works in my queue. Most were self-help, educational, or business related. When I tackled them, I found that if you read the first and last paragraph of each chapter and subchapter you will gain the point of what they are teaching. The middle part is typically anecdotal: for some concepts that I did not grasp I would read this portion to understand, and for the ones I grasped I would skip over the middle. I also found that I could integrate this process while playing poker online. So now I was still doing my work but tackling multiple tasks at the same time.

I have already mentioned that multitasking is not completely optimal, and so it seemed that what I was doing would have a negative effect. I would not be focused on the game, and that would hurt me, and because my attention would be divided from the reading, I would not be retaining all the information. There may be some merit to this, so I carefully weighed the expected value. If my poker playing and reading combo were negative, by how much? I calculated that it was likely that reading would take away 10 percent of my focus and that playing poker would also have a 10 percent reduction in my retention. This was marginal to me, and the time spent doing them separately was more costly than doing them together. You cannot get time back, and it's our most valuable commodity, remember? The results were fascinating. I maintained my win rate in poker and was flying through books.

Now as far as books go, if someone reads them cover to cover and takes five hours to do so, but I read it my way in an hour, what is the difference? The one who takes five hours would likely get an A on a test, but I could likely get a C or B. So I am retaining close to 80 percent of the book's insight versus the five-hour guy who retains 90 percent. In that five hours, though, I can have 80 percent of five books compared to 90 percent of one book. I like my way better and here is why. One book will not change your life; it may inspire you, but wouldn't 80 percent still inspire you on a close enough level to have the same effect? Books are merely a tool, and the mechanic who has the bigger tool box is more likely to help you with more problems than one with a really good hammer. There were some days when I wanted to give up and thought, "This is silly. I don't need to do this," but I had made a commitment to this experiment and held true to it.

A few weeks in, my body had changed, and a six pack that I never knew I could have had emerged. My brain had become flooded with new ideas, concepts, and inspiration. When I was faced with doubt I remained disciplined, and this was the greatest by-product of this process. I made a goal, achieved it, and learned how to discipline myself. At the end of the 67 days, my body looked better than it had ever looked, I felt smarter and noticed that when I talked to people, I was able to add more because I had read about so many topics that made me more well-rounded. All it took was a decision to experiment, and the reason I was able to do so was in part because of the practice I have had for years behind the bar. Knowing that there was always an opportunity to use my other hand to be more efficient helped me integrate all of these new notions and integrate them in an optimal fashion.

You may be sitting there saying to yourself, I am not a bartender, how does this apply to me? You can come up with many excuses not to do something if you look for them, but you can also come up with just as many reasons to do something important as well. Approach your life like the bartender approaches his work. Use this as a model not a rule, and you can find that you too can optimize your potential and success. I would argue that I am the most optimal, successful bartender there is. I am not the fastest in the world, but I am close, and I do not make the most money, but I make the most that I can where I am. I have always considered making the move to the top bartending gigs out there, but the reality for me is that even if I were the best bartender in the world it is not my destiny or dream. However, I will be the best I can be where I am because this attitude leaks into other more important areas in my life.

You may be in a job that you do not like and have aspirations to do something different. Most bartenders fall into this category, but most do not work hard where they are, and that becomes their makeup that keeps them from doing better in other areas. Are you doing the best you can at your job even if you hate it? If the answer is no, then ponder this. If I gave you all that you wanted, for instance a million dollars, would that make you successful?

The honest answer is no.

That is why so many people who come into instant wealth do not keep it. They do not know how they got it, thus they do not know how to keep it. You may say that this is not you and that with this gift you would be able to keep it and grow it. I have never had a green thumb, but I assure you that if I didn't have a good work ethic and humility, I would end up allowing weeds to grow and kill whatever beautiful garden I was given.

Why? Because I know nothing about it, and without preparation, study, and the correct mindset, my efforts would be all for naught. When you can work hard at a job you do not like, then you can move mountains in areas you do like. Think about this concept: if you are willing to recognize that work is work no matter your level of appeal, and you can move past this to do the best you can, then when you add passion it will create a recipe for success. I enjoy bartending, but I love being a poker player and entrepreneur. When I leave the bar after knowing I worked as hard as I could, I can't wait to use that momentum in the areas I truly love.

A bartender's word of advice—"One of the greatest gifts you will receive in life is knowledge. It may be to do this or not do that, but the distinction will allow you to become optimal, make fewer mistakes, and always remember your purpose in life."

CHAPTER TEN

Golden Handcuffs

Bartending has become my golden handcuffs. It is a great job that provides a good living, comfort, and freedom to live a life that I want. However, it is a trap for me that breeds comfort in myself and many others in this profession. Many people find themselves in these types of jobs. They say that they would pursue their dreams but that they make a good living and have security. First of all, this is a myth. In today's world there is no such thing as security. We are told that if you go to college, get a good job, and work hard, you will be rewarded. This was true decades ago, but times have changed. The numbers are in, and the value of the hard worker with seniority has passed us by. It is not fair, but such is life, right? You work hard do a good job and then, boom, downsizing, or they fire you with a pathetic severance in favor of the younger guy. Why is this?

Here is what is going on. You have worked for 10 years, and say you make 40k a year, and you are the best in your position. We will say you are a factory worker. You have dedicated the last 10 years of your life missing holidays, working overtime, basically giving your life to this company, so you think it is unfair that they let you go. Now you have to find a job, and times are tough. It is not fair you believe, but here is why they do it: you are replaceable. Even Steve Jobs was replaced from his OWN company that he started! It actually makes sense to fire you mathematically. They can hire two people for the same price as you, and sure, they may only be 75 percent as skilled, but two people at that level versus you at 100 percent still leaves them being more productive. It is cost effective to let you go.

I too fell into this category as head bartender. I did not get fired, but my ego told me that there was no way the bar could manage without me. It was not until my friend got fired from his bartending job at which he had worked for 10 years as the head bartender that I realized my ego was blinding me. I was replaceable, and the bar would continue with or without me. Sure, in the short term, there could be a drop in business and productivity, but overall, it would still be profitable and be just fine if I were let go. When I finally left The Waterfront I saw this first hand. Was I the best bartender? Without a doubt! Did that bar close after I left? NO WAY. If you can be humble enough to realize this then you can do something about it. Prepare for the next step. If you can get fired from a job you hate wouldn't it be better to get fired from a job you love? Never get comfortable. You may think you are happy, but comfort and happiness are not the same. If you are not going to go to work tap dancing, then you need to get out of your comfort zone and look for your next move as would a master chess player. Sure, you will have to sacrifice just like you would a pawn, but as long as you are moving forward with a plan then those sacrifices will be worth it.

There is one constant in life, and for me it is math. If the math is there, it is hard to argue. In poker I rely on math more than feeling. People believe that poker is all about reading your opponent, but no matter how skilled you are at this, you will never have definite answers but only educated guesses. I use the math because in the law of averages my decisions will be profitable. This leads me to my very own golden handcuffs of bartending. Many people ask me why I bartend when I have a degree, a wealth of knowledge, and talents. Why am I wasting my time when I could be doing greater things?

They cannot see the bigger picture; it's not that I do not agree with them, but they only see one side of the cube. They do not see the endless hours I spend on poker, myself, and my other endeavors. However, it is very hard for me to walk away from the bar because of math. Let me show you mathematically what I mean that patrons are unaware of. Could I get a day job that society deems professional and even admirable? Of course, but I say why? Even you may be nodding your head, but here is why I do not do that. First of all, I do not want a job; I want something more. I want to be my own boss and create something larger than life that also affects others in a positive way, such as this book. That doesn't happen just by taking a job more often than not. As for the math, let us see what kind of job I would have to get to make it mathematically better for me to leave the bar or to even be comparable.

Ready for some math? I'll make it easy for you. I take home about 50k a year; that's after taxes! Not a ton of money, but higher than the average, so given that taxes usually take about 35 percent of your income, that actually means I make about 80k a year. That sounds like a pretty good yearly income, right? I only work 25 hours a week, whereas most work 50 hours, and that may not even include their commute. In Los Angeles, many people spend 10 to 15 hours a week commuting, but for this we will say 50 total hours committed to their job. So if I were to take a full time job that requires 50 hours a week, this means that in order to make the same amount I would have to take a job that starts at 160k a year.

Oh, I forgot, I take a lot of time off whenever I want. Last year alone I spent a week in Hong Kong, a week in Macau, a week in the Dominican Republic, a week in Cancun, a week in New Orleans, and a week in North Carolina. That is not including a few quick trips I took just on a whim. That is almost two months of vacation time! What job allows you that while still clearing 50k? I also play poker full time and make a decent amount every year from that, but it also requires time away from the bar including four weeks during the World Series of Poker in Las Vegas. I can't really make a justifiable number for how much this is worth because it is hard to place a value I receive from these experiences. Let us say that I succumb to the two weeks of vacation time most of you look forward to. I would then estimate that I would need a job that starts at 200k to warrant leaving the bar job behind me.

Now, you may say this is ridiculous, but you have to look at it through a new set of eyes. Obviously a job that would even pay me 100k would mean more money, but the amount of time to earn that would mean I would actually be taking a cut in my hourly wages and, more importantly to me, in my life value. I hope you can see that when you really break down your situation it can become clearer. The people who ask me why I do not take a job like theirs do not see the full spectrum, and that's fine; they do not have to because it is my life. While I may have the golden handcuffs firmly in place, they do not keep my hands from working. What they do not see behind the scenes is that the freedom bartending allows gives way for me to pursue my passions. Some of you may have these golden handcuffs but are also stuck in your own self-inflicted prison. Amber's story may look similar to yours.

When I dated Amber, I believe that she fell in love with me in part because I was the type of person she wanted to be. One issue was that she was not of the right mindset to be like me or embrace the lifestyle and mindset that I have cultivated over the years. She was a project manager for a great company. This was actually a company that is rare in today's society. Her future was paved right in front of her; she would certainly have security and move up the ladder and would likely never get fired. She was already making a little over six figures but HATED her job. She went to school for psychology and was passionate about it, but with student loans and the need for a job, she took the safe route, which most do and probably most should because they don't have that drive inside them that does not listen to fears. She grew up with parents who were from the old society: they had good jobs, worked hard, and were going to be just fine in retirement. This was the path she found herself on, and I believe she will have the same life as they did and will one day retire comfortably.

FUCK comfort!

I don't like being comfortable because that means I am not growing and that my life is dictated by someone else. Obviously this is where we differed despite a potential desire within her to be like I was. You already know the story whereby I tried to conform to her insecurities and need for comfort and security, but I went through Hurricane Katrina, and I couldn't do it. I know that the best plan can still be destroyed and that we will all face our own versions of Katrina.

Amber started off as an analyst under a very laid-back boss. He allowed her to take time off whenever she wanted, come in late and leave early, and really have little responsibilities. She could work from home and get paid when she wasn't there, and she had great benefits. She was not challenged in this position. Her job was in human resources, where she barely used her degree, one that she was passionate about and wanted to use. We all make choices, and she was faced with one when the position for project manager came across her desk. She would earn almost 20k more a year, but she would actually have to work hard, time off would be a challenge, and she would have to go in early and come home late, which was never the case in her then current positon. In fact, she usually went in late to beat the traffic and left early while usually enjoying a two-hour lunch break. When we discussed this opportunity, I told her flat out it was a mistake. Sure, you want to grow and move up, but was it really worth it? I didn't think so. Why would you now commit more time and effort to a career you really didn't want, and looking at the math she really wouldn't be making more money when you factor in the extra hours and lack of time off. What drove her to take the new position was a poor perspective and the wrong kind of drive within her. She wanted to have more responsibilities because she thought she was supposed to. It was natural progression. Work hard, move up. This was instilled within her by her upbringing, and there was no way I could change decades of this mindset—she took the job.

SHE WAS MISERABLE!

I knew it. I tried to show her, but a miscalculating cognitive bias made the decision for her. We are all on a path, but is it the right path? My perspective said no; she was trading in a lot of life value for what, 20 to 30k more. You can't put a price on that. She had found yoga and fallen in love with it to the point that amid this new job we discussed opening up a yoga studio. I was in full support of this idea, but it was too scary for her and with our other relationship issues we broke up before we could explore this possibility further.

Ironically, after we had been apart I found out that she indeed opened up a yoga studio with her new boyfriend. At first I was pissed off; it seemed that she was finally using some of the ideas and tools I tried so hard to give her. I quickly released these egocentric feelings and was happy for her. However, this was not a happy ending but a learning lesson for you. In my opinion she did it half assed, but I only know a little bit about the situation, so I can only speculate. She opened her studio, but it was only open a few hours a night and would close within a year. She got engaged and moved to Oregon with her future husband. Her closing down the yoga studio and taking a job similar to the one she had had led me to contemplate how this could have possibly happened. I can only think that if she had quit her job and really put in the effort she could have, without a doubt, had a successful business. When you only pursue your dreams part time, you will get part-time success. She was successful in opening her studio, her dream, but was unable to embrace the insecurity of the endeavor and thus let her dream slip away. Now, I only know a small part of the details so I like to think that maybe the studio was not what she had envisioned and it was more important for her to raise a family with her future husband than to have a business. There is nothing wrong with this decision, and I hope that her path is one of happiness, but use this as a lesson that you can simulate and learn from without having to go through the mistakes yourself and lose time.

If you are in a job that gives the impression of security, but it keeps you from going all in on your dreams, ask if this is the true value of your life. Is this all you want from life, to play it safe and just get by? If it is, then who am I to say you're wrong, but if it is not, and for most people this is the case, then go all in. What Amber never realized was that the type of job she had would always be there. She could have gone all in, failed, and then retreated back. But because she didn't go all in, she will likely never be satisfied and have no real closure. Again, maybe it doesn't matter for her, but it matters to me and probably you.

"The richest place in the world is the graveyard."

I heard Les Brown say that over and over, and I am sure he got it from somewhere else, but don't let your vision and even more so your dreams keep you company when you're six-feet under. Make sure you finish this race of life completely exhausted and left without any thoughts of could have, should have, or would have.

Make the golden handcuffs your choice as a means to an end, but don't use your hands to build a prison. Use them to cultivate what you are truly passionate about. If I am a bartender for the rest of my life, I will not see that as a failure as long as I know I have had my all-in moments. I have been all in on poker for years, and for me the time is growing close that I may have to end the experiment. It is not because I don't believe that I can achieve my goals as a world champion but because I know that despite giving it my all it may not be in the cards. I chose a passion that is unfair and does not always reward the best. But I chose it and have given it my all and continue to do so as I write this. I have found that I have other passions that are just as great and can offer more to this world than being a poker champ could ever provide. I will never stop playing, but I may divert my focus to something else when the time is right.

Sometimes in life it is when we stop wanting something that it finally comes to us. There is a poker pro named Will Failla who did not win a world title until he was in his forties. He had played for decades and time and again he came up short. I have had the honor of playing with him, and he inspires me to never give up on my dreams. With this said, he has other endeavors that he pursues and has had success that has kept him in the game he loves. For me, this is bartending, but as time goes by I know that I will achieve my dreams. It may not be a poker title, but I have many dreams. As long as I chase them, the ones that are meant to be will be and those that are not will at least leave me knowing that I went for them and not leave me wondering. Poker has been a gift to me, and many have asked when I would hang it up since to them it's obvious that it's just not going to happen. Over the years I have never had a losing year. I am ahead in the game over my lifetime, but I want to ask you, how often do you have a legitimate shot at taking home over 500k in a week?

Every year I play, I have this opportunity more than a dozen times, and when I am ready I will have that moment. To win a title and take home life changing money is what keeps me focused on this dream every day. What recently was revealed to me through my own self-reflection were these ridiculous notions:

"I am too busy" or

"I don't have enough time."

I used to say these things, like most of us do, until I realized that they were the biggest lies I could ever tell myself. Just like multitasking behind the bar, I realized in my life I was capable of doing so much more concurrently while I bartended and played poker. I thought the answer was keeping it simple. There is some truth to this notion, but for me, and hopefully you, the idea that I could always do more resonated with me. There are 24 hours in the day—are you using them optimally? I was not. I found that every second that I wasted watching TV, playing video games, or simply meandering through life was taking me away from my goals and not toward them. When I feel this coming on or notice I am being wasteful, I quickly get uncomfortable, and that's when I get back to work.

We all need to sleep, and some of us say they cannot function on less than eight hours. When you are driven, you will forget to sleep and even eat sometimes. It happens to me all the time. When I have to go work at the bar I go in at six and get off at two am. Most go home and pass out; I come home and read my book of the day, play poker as long as I can, and when that is over, I write. Many times I do not go to bed until six am, sometimes later, but I wake up by noon, and more often than not, earlier. My phone rings and wakes me up because I need to make plans to meet with mentors or others whom I can look to in helping me pursue my goals. I always answer my phone because when it rings that is opportunity, and I cannot ignore it. I have pulled a lot of all-nighters and had to rely on a few hours or a short nap. That is all I have time for, and I do it because my want is greater than my excuses. I want to break out of the golden handcuffs and create a life greater than my imagination. Why spend time sleeping and dreaming about it when I can be awake living it?

It was said that Beyonce once stayed up for three days and forgot to eat the whole time because she was working so hard. It sounds ridiculous, but what is more ridiculous is to not see that this was a small sacrifice to achieve her dreams. It was the desire that fueled her to not give into nature's simple desires.

Fifty Cent was once asked when he slept, and he responded, "Sleep? Sleep is for those people who are broke. I don't sleep. I might miss the opportunity to make a dream a reality."

Sleep is just another form of golden handcuffs; it makes you comfortable. Bartending can make me comfortable if I choose to allow it. Sleep is just a metaphor that represents everything that keeps you from your goals and desires. Do not let the golden cuffs hold you prisoner; melt them down and invest in yourself.

A bartender's word of advice—"We are constantly swept away in the currents of life that will lead us in the direction that they flow whether we want to go downstream or not. The salmon swims upstream in order to spawn because its desire is inherent. To spawn your life, follow the salmon, not the debris that is prisoner to the confines of the current."

169

CHAPTER ELEVEN

The 99 Percent and Opportunities

By now you are obviously able to see that the bar is a metaphor for life. It is a place that provides good times, memories, and life lessons. You will find all walks of life inside a bar, and I see them daily. Everyone you encounter, just like in life, will provide a lesson for you should you choose to be willing to learn. Business deals and meetings are conducted, all forms of partnerships are realized, and lessons of caution are commonplace—and you have been exposed to them all. Maybe you were unaware, but hopefully some of what I have shared with you has not necessarily been a new concept; rather it has opened your eyes to things that were not clearly visible. The majority of bar goers consist of the 99 percent. We have been confronted through the media by this concept and the idea that the one percent is against us. I don't take sides on this matter, and both sides are valid in their opinions and concepts, but I do have a different way of looking at this concept that will make you think.

We should stop blaming the one percent and perceiving them as evil. They are taking advantage of life and constructing how the 99 percent lives. What is shocking is while the 99 are blaming, they are not realizing that they are allowing the one percent to take advantage of them. As a bartender I am amongst the 99, but I do not believe the one percenters are taking advantage of me; instead, I believe that they are seizing opportunities. It is up to me to adhere to the societal norms they are influencing should I choose to do so. From my position behind the bar I can see the full scope of man and all their differences and limiting beliefs. While the guy grinding his way through life at his average job complains about taxes and life not being fair, he is wasting his time, and no one really cares. The one percent are not the reason you are not successful or that you cannot afford certain luxuries that you desire. The person complaining can look no further than himself to place blame. While he cries and wallows in the idea of life not being fair, the one percent is putting in the time and optimizing their vision and income.

You may ask yourself why you are not driving a Ferrari or living in a mansion in Beverly Hills, but counter that and ask, am I doing what those who have those things are doing? If the answer is no, then you have no reason to feel sorry for yourself or blame others. Do you have an investor's mentality? Probably not. It is the harsh reality of the 99 percent and the one percent, and all the ad agencies know this. They paint a picture of desire that makes us feel "less than." If we had these things we would be happy, but we don't, so we are supposed to be miserable. Drink this if you want, but I choose not to because I know that I am where I am because of the mindset I have placed myself in. The one percent calls the shots in our society because they have the money and the power.

Life is not fair, so this concept may not be, but it's up to you to accept it and do something about it because nothing will come from just complaining and blaming. We are constantly bombarded with how life should be and what we should want, but we allow ourselves to be brainwashed, so that means it is our fault. Big companies use ads that create insecurities and desires that are not real. When they do this, they make money off of us because they need us to overextend ourselves and stay in debt. The idea of a savings account has been preached to us since banks became commonplace. We put our money in a savings account and falsely believe we are doing the right thing. The reality is that we barely save what we should, and even the best account will only garner a five percent return on our money. That is almost impossible to find, and as I write this most only provide a rate of 0.01. That is insane! With inflation, we are really just holding on to our money rather than growing it. The banks take our money and invest. For example, they take your money and loan it out for a mortgage, which creates more debt, and thus they get a larger return the longer the debt is present. Let that sink in; they are taking your money and making money off of it.

Why can't you be the bank? I am not saying open up a bank, but what I am saying is look for better ways to invest your money, and do not adhere to what has been told to you by companies that are trying to make money off of you. The first rule of saving money is to eliminate debt; the second is to invest. I don't have a formula for how to make money for you, but what I can provide is the opportunity to adopt a new mindset once you realize that the majority of what the media tells you is their motive for keeping you as a consumer.

Reality shows are ruining people left and right and not just because of their mind-numbing programming but because of what they are subconsciously selling. Who creates these shows? That's right, the one percent. I understand the idea of tuning out and the entertainment factor they provide; hell, I watch them too (they can be hilarious). However, when people watch the

Kardashians, there is more going on than simple entertainment, and the producers know it. We believe that when we watch their lives on screen that we should be entitled to the same lifestyle. What they forget to mention is that there was a lot of hard work that went into getting them to where they are. You can argue that Kim Kardashian did nothing to be famous, and I could agree. Her family, just like the Hiltons, put in a lot of hard work, and they are the beneficiaries of past success. You cannot compete with good genes, but you can create good genes for yourself and your future generations by putting in the work that Conrad Hilton and Bruce Jenner did.

Hilton was a fighter and never gave up in order to forge his empire, while Bruce worked his ass off to be an Olympic champion. We do not hear much about this and only see the fruits of their labors. I will even challenge the idea of Kim Kardashian and her entitlement. She was blessed with admirable physical attributes, and certainly her inheritance gave her a leg up on the game, but what she did with the opportunities has made her an investor in life and, as we see, very wealthy. She could have just sat back and lived off the fruits of her family, but she created an empire, and every time we watch that show, it is one big ad that makes her money from going to her stores or advertising dollars on her ratings. You are making her rich by wanting to be like her, and she knows it and thus exploits it. It is our responsibility to be aware of this and not let it dictate our lives. I will not argue whether or not Kim or Paris Hilton are good role models or even smart; that's easily debatable. However, they must be smart to have seized the opportunities when they were presented, and more so, to have known who to align themselves with in order to maximize their profits and exposure.

Rather than blame the one percent, become the one percent if you want that for your life. If you do not, then be happy for them and accepting of yourself, but know that the bed you make is the one you CHOOSE to lie in at night. I have had the privilege of meeting many successful and very wealthy people in my life. The first thing I notice is that they are all confident, some arrogant, but overall just confident. They had a vision and would not stop until they realized it. We have this myth that people are overnight successes, but this is an apparition not a rule. Bill Gates talks about the 10 dark years when he was so focused on his vision in which he did not take one day off, not one!

How many times during that 10 years do you think he spent sitting at a bar blaming the one percent for his not being where he wanted to be? I would say zero because his mindset was that if it is possible for others to succeed, then I am no different. We are all the same, and yes, some of us get a head start with the work that our families did before us, but understand that at one point someone had to work. Those of this fabric will lose this wealth if they do not continue to work, but their other advantage is that they have people around them who can show them the way, be it within their family or circle of friends. There is a scientific notion that if your five closest friends are overweight, within two years you to will find yourself overweight. It may not be an absolute law, but think about it and how true it can be. Those whom you spend the majority of your time around will influence you for better or worse. If they are overweight you may stop working out as much or start eating like them because of their influence. Now, if you spent your time with successful people who were in a position in life that you admire, you will begin to adopt their traits and mimic them. I do not mean that you must abandon your old friends for rich ones. Simply know that the influence of others is strong, and your mind will play tricks on you and lead you to believe that you are just fine. If you wanted to be a successful doctor and spent all of your time with accountants you will be limiting your potential to become a great doctor. I spend the majority of my time with like-minded people who want more out of life than those who are content with the daily grind. They influence me positively and make me strive for more, even challenging me daily whenever I find myself becoming lethargic. You may not have been born into wealth and may be a step behind, but that doesn't mean you can't change your situation.

When I was young, I went to private school despite my parents having to go into debt just to afford that opportunity. It was not a given that I would be smarter or even successful in life, but it was a good starting point. The sacrifice that my parents made gave me more opportunities in life. When you make any sacrifice in life for an opportunity, you can be presented with the opportunity to be successful. I graduated from a public high school with a class of 200. Fewer than 50 of those whom I graduated with went to a four-year college, so roughly 25 percent. Most of them did not have the foundation of a private school, and where I grew up, the private schools had the better teachers and typically produced better students. Of the 25 students in my last year of private school, more than half went on to a four-year college. This is an example that if you are surrounded by like-minded people you will likely find yourself being similar.

In contrast, I had a friend named Luke whom I grew up with who went to public school. Luke was very smart and one of the best chess players I had ever played against. I taught him the game, and he quickly took to it. At the time I was arguably the best player in our area. He had the skills to be successful; however, at school he was friends with peers who did not challenge him and held him back. We grew up across the street from one another and while there are many reasons that led to him dropping out of school, I believe one major reason was because of who he was surrounded by. He chose to spend his time with lesser companions and be a victim of his circumstance rather than spend his time with me or other friends of value.

Childhood has many obstacles and issues in itself and while he didn't have some of the opportunities I benefited from due to my parents and friends, it did not have to be his reality. It was his own choosing in the end that led him to where he is today. He had the intellect, but had no one there to help him grow. He has many reasons to blame his surroundings, but in the end he chose to stay in the bed he was given because it was easier to blame than to accept and change. No matter the real reason he became a dropout, in the end, who really paid the price for those he chose to spend his time with or his mindset and victim mentality? At the end of the day, you have to look yourself in the mirror and realize that all the choices we make we must be held accountable for.

Do not believe the idea that you have no choice. A choice is always being made even when you feel like it is not up to you. The reason is because you have a choice to accept it or to do something about it. What is your value scale? Is it more important to look successful than actually to be successful? Is it more important to be cool rather than to take the harder classes to better your life? Is it more important to sit at the bar watching ESPN or to stay home studying or working on yourself? What we value makes our decisions for us. Here in LA we probably have more BMWs and Mercedes Benzes than any other city in the country. It is a status symbol that is valued when we know that there are plenty of cheaper, more effective cars on the road. The mindset of those who own these cars is that the car means they are successful. It is just a car, but the media has made this notion true. People will buy a car they can't really afford because of image rather than reality. Let the status exude from within not from the opinions of others.

Luke thought it was more important to be cool and have "fun" rather than put the work in. He now pays for it every day of his life, and without cultivating a strong mental foundation he will likely continue on this path until he dies. When he reaches this point, there will be plenty of people there to say it was not his fault and he could have or would have been this or that had he been placed in a better situation. This is valid but not important because inevitably it was his life and his design that failed. In the end he will only be able to blame one person, himself.

The bar is full of Lukes because it is a place to escape from the reality of our own design. Certainly successful people come in; in fact, Elon Musk once came into my bar. To be honest, I would have never noticed him had someone not pointed out who he was. He didn't come in wearing a top-of-the-line tailored suit, just a T-shirt and jeans. His company SpaceX was celebrating a launch and enjoying their success. Many of the employees come in day after day, and just like this day they were partying as expected.

A guy came up to me and told me to get him a drink, saying, "Don't you know who he is? Drop what you're doing."

I didn't bat an eye or drool over Elon, and ironically all he wanted was water. He was a regular guy, although his intellect and bank account, to his employees, would say otherwise. He wanted to be treated like a normal guy, and I think that in our brief interaction he appreciated this. In fact, the way his employees idolized him made him uncomfortable. What was more amazing to me was the fact that on this amazing day, a day where his vision had been realized, he chose to celebrate with water, unlike his employees. I believe this is why he is who he is and his employees are who they are. All of them are intelligent; hell, to launch a rocket you have to be a rocket scientist, and most that night were. Some of the smartest minds in the city in one place, and yet one man stood above them. While today was a success, and it made sense to celebrate like his employees, deep down Elon knew the value of his time, and I have no doubt that partying that night would have taken away from what he was going to do the following day.

As a former athlete, I have read how some of the greatest basketball players would win a game and then still shoot around for hours after the game because they valued getting better more than the victories. Amazing—you just won a game and yet you stay in the gym to work. What a great mindset and one that separates the winners in life. It comes back to what you value. Many times we value things or achievements but we overlook the real prize, which is progress. When you want to get off the barstool and become an Elon Musk of the world, you will realize that winners in life strive for progress, not perfection. Perfection only lasts for a moment if it even exists at all. Being perfect is boring because once you get to the top of the mountain there is only one direction to go and that's down. However, reaching the top of any mountain can be done, but there are always mountains to climb. It is always the pursuit that drives us and we will reflect on more than the view from the top, no matter how sweet it is.

A bartender's word of advice—"When you feel that all your prayers would be answered if you had this or that, smash this notion and revise your plan. Your plan is what you can control, and as my father always told me, 'If frogs had wings they wouldn't bump their ass every time they jumped.'" -

CHAPTER TWELVE

A Sober Reality

This may come as a shock, but I am a sober bartender and have been since I came to LA. It was not my plan, but it became my reality a few short weeks after I moved. Most people will offer to buy me drinks, especially shots, and I decline. I do not offer this insight liberally, but when pressed I tell those who inquire that I am working or that I am allergic. Of course, many bartenders partake, so when I use the work excuse, it is more often than not challenged. I find it comical; what job would condone drinking? However, it has been commonly accepted in my field. As for the allergy, I make light of it saying that when I drink I tend to lose my clothes, which is true. I did a lot of streaking in my day. For those who continue to press, I reveal my secret that I am sober. This strikes them as if they were looking at a unicorn. It seems unfathomable that one could bartend without drinking, but I assure you it can be done and is done by myself and many others.

I have encountered some confrontation from managers and owners at first, but typically they are relieved because I am always reliable, and it's certainly more profitable since many bartenders take liberties with the inventory. Like all life changes, something had to spawn this transformation in me. So here is my story.

When I came to LA I thought that I had put my life back together following the depression I went through after Katrina. I was highly functioning, but something inside me for my whole life was able to mask certain issues that would constantly take a toll on me without my even being aware. When I arrived in LA, I knew that I was a heavy drinker but no different than most of the company I kept, and in many circumstances I was actually a lightweight. I knew that in coming to LA there would be a lot of pressure to survive and that I was all in, especially after that fireside discussion with my parents. I knew that I was on my own and that drinking would have to take a back seat in order to make it in LA. I did not want to be one of the many stories that are all too commonplace. Thousands of people are chewed up and spit out within a year of coming to LA, and I was hell-bent on being one of the successful ones; however, my path to success would have to be different and one that I was unaware of.

As many stories begin, it all started with a girl whom I do not blame but am thankful for because she was the straw that broke this camel's back. I mentioned this story earlier but intentionally left out one of the keys to my success. The greatest gift my DUI gave me was that of sobriety. If you recall the story that led to "my life being over" then you will recall what led me to this moment. I told you the work I put, in but the foundation was forged that day in the lawyer's office. The last thing he told me before I left was that in order to avoid jail time for my actions I should attend AA meetings, start a log of all the meetings I went to, and when we went in front of the judge, admit I had a problem but that I was doing something about it. I was not ready to admit I had a drinking problem; I was young and made a mistake, but that aside, I knew that whatever it took to survive, I would do and I would listen. I wrote a plan that night and vowed to execute it. I needed to get a job, a bike, go to meetings to get mercy from the judge, and save every penny just to eat.

Life had forced me to leave the highest point in my life in New Orleans, and now I had made a poor decision that put me behind the eight ball, but neither had killed me, even though I believe that I had flirted with death and dodged it. I was hustling, looking for jobs and trying to survive on my financed bike until the day finally came that I would go to my first AA meeting. It was a cold and rainy February night, and the meeting was a few miles away as I tucked my jeans in my socks and pedaled my way to the meeting in order to start my log.

I sat in the back and listened to a woman named Virginia share her story of being a country club wife drinking gin and tonics and blacking out at PTA meetings. We had nothing in common, or so I thought. When they asked who was new, I raised my hand for some reason, and when asked if I was an alcoholic, I said I was not sure, much to their amusement. At the end of the meeting, I went to get my sheet signed, and people surrounded me. They were so interested in my story; no matter what I said they all seemed genuine, and most nodded their head as if to say, "Yes, I too have that tale in my repertoire."

They gave me the Book of Alcoholics Anonymous for free, which I stuffed in my pants and made way toward my bike.

A few men came up to me and said, "It's raining. We can take you home. We have a truck and can toss your bike in the back."

I replied, "Nope, I'm good," and refused their help.

It is a story that is told throughout the halls of AA here in LA. I was so filled with unbridle pride that in my lowest moments I would not accept help.

All I wanted was to fill my sheet so I wouldn't go to jail, but more importantly, I wanted them to prove that I was not one of them, which was easy to do as all I focused on were the differences. I would attend a few more meetings in the area since it was the shortest bike ride, and I saw a lot of familiar faces that were always friendly and never pressuring. They were simply there, ready to help, but accepting that it had to be on my timeline.

February 22, 2006, I was at a meeting in which I had become comfortable and started to actually enjoy. Going to meetings actually made me feel better about myself because a lot of people had it way worse than I did. I know that sounds a bit sadistic, but at least I was getting something out of it other than a simple signature. Little did I know at the time, but this would be a life changing night. It did not come with a grand gesture or parting of the seas. I had read the book they gave me and listened during the meetings in order to figure their program out so that I could convince myself that I was not like them and did not have a problem. It had worked, but after that meeting a guy grabbed me to the side before I could slip out.

His name was Bill, and to this day I do not know if he is sober, dead, or drinking, but he changed my life. I have never seen him since that night, but he posed one question that challenged me.

He said, "So when are you going to get sober?"

I had continued drinking at this point, although not to the degree I had been accustomed to because I had to prove to myself that I did not have a problem.

I responded, "Monday sounds like a good idea."

He laughed, shook his head, and said, "See, I knew you couldn't do it, else you would start today."

I was enraged. Who did this guy think he was? He doesn't know me. I'll show him, I thought.

I said, "Fine, today it is."

Boy, did he trick me, but with that one moment my life changed and along with it, my path.

I started my sobriety date but without the notion that I was an alcoholic. My grandfather and father were alcoholics. My grandfather drank himself to death, and my father had a moment of clarity and stopped drinking one day after my mother threatened to leave him. My father had my mother and me to considered, but all I had was myself, and so the only person I was responsible for was looking me in the mirror. I owed it to my reflection to give it a shot in order to survive. It made financial sense, and I knew that in order to make it, I needed to try something different. I was willing to listen even if my true motivation was not pure.

I would stay sober and still do to this day because of one word, POTENTIAL. Whether or not I was an alcoholic in your opinion or my definition did not matter; I had the potential to epitomize that definition, which was reason enough and has been to motivate me to maintain a sober life. A few weeks of sobriety went by, and I felt better and started losing weight, but honestly this was a scam. I was doing it until I got my life back in order and would leave these meetings and all those who were so kind to help me in the dust, until one evening when I met Gary.

Gary was the speaker at a meeting one night, and I had never seen him before. He had 15 years sober, and when he began I went on autopilot, as I figured his story would not be mine and it would soon be over. A few minutes in, he caught my attention when he said he had moved to LA to be in the entertainment industry and worked as a bartender, a job he kept though his sobriety.

HE HAD MY STORY!

Damn, I thought, I was no longer unique, and someone had been on the path I was currently on. He came up to me and gave me his number after the meeting. As I was preparing for my bike ride home someone checked in with me and asked if I had found a sponsor, someone to guide me through this program. This of course was the last thing I wanted, as it might jeopardize my scam, but on the ride home I thought Gary would be perfect. Many people in the program told me I was doomed if I bartended, but here was a guy who proved that theory wrong. More importantly, I did not see him at many meetings, so if I asked him to sponsor me it would probably not be much of a commitment.

I called Gary the next day, and he agreed to be my sponsor. He told me to call him every day and we would go to a meeting together every week. Not exactly what I had in mind, but it seemed easy enough. We talked every day and forged a beautiful friendship but more so a mentorship on how to live a sober but good life. Gary never asked anything of me other than to stay sober and work on myself for me not for him. There was something inside me that wanted what he had. He had a great job, a beautiful house, a great relationship with his partner, and everyone seemed to love him—all the things I wanted.

Here is the irony: I heard a few things in his speech that I connected with him, believing we were the same, but we were not. He did not grow up where I did, did not go to the same schools as me, and to my surprise, he was gay. I did not have much contact with homosexuals but did not really have any opinion of them. However, when I found this out I fell back into that poor way of thinking that looked at the differences and not the similarities. This was quickly smashed because Gary was teaching me that this was not advantageous and a poor way of looking at life. If we look at the similarities we will be able to connect, and connection is the key to a happy life. There are not many happy rich hermits in this world. I did not want to be a hermit, and if I wanted a life better than the one I had, I needed to take direction. That was a turning point for me.

Gary said to me, "We are different, and you may not want the life I have, or maybe you only desire a few elements, but no matter the reason ask yourself this: do you like the life you have? Your entire life you have been the director in this film called life, and this is where it has led you. Maybe it's time to be the actor and take direction because you have been trying to do the directing, acting, producing, etc., all on your own, and you have failed."

This shook me to the core, but there was an important element that you should be aware of. If I had not been at a place in my life and had a psyche of willingness, his words would have fallen on deaf ears. It took me going through Katrina and crashing my car to finally reach a point of willingness to admit that I needed help in life. Being a giant can only come by sitting on the shoulders of giants, and I was ready. They say when the student is ready the master will appear. Gary was the first, and I have been fortunate enough to find many masters and will continue to seek more as I go on. He was the first in my sobriety, but once sober, I learned that it was not simply good enough to stop drinking.

In order to have a good life I would have to face all of my fears and resentments and embrace them so that I could learn from them in order to become a better person. Sobriety in the beginning is about the drink, but once you remove the drink you have to deal with yourself without any distractions, which is what drinking is. It is a distraction so that you do not have to feel, at least that is how I used it. Did I wake up in the morning needing a drink or always drink to blackout? NO, that was not my story, and to be honest, if you saw me drinking you would likely laugh at the notion that I even had a problem with it. What I did have was a problem with life. That is why I would drink, and many times it was subconscious. It was not until I had some time sober that I realized this truth. Many will never realize it because they will not experience any profound duration of sobriety. How many times do we say I could do this or I could do that, I just do not want to. I challenge that notion wholeheartedly because you are playing a fool's game. I always thought I could stop drinking but had never stopped. My arrogance told me that I could if I wanted to, but it wasn't until I actually did something about it that I could have the right to say yes I can.

I understand this may sound odd coming from someone who works in and loves bars. I do not stand on a soapbox preaching for people to get sober, but for those who may have this idea or even desire I feel it is important that I show that it is an option. Obviously it could hurt my wallet if everyone got sober, but for those who are at this crossroads, I hope that I can be an example, and for those who are bold enough to inquire, I can help. Many have approached me about being sober as they down drink after drink. It is not my position to drag them out of their comfort zone, but when they are willing I will be as well. I have taken people from the bar to meetings, many of which have not been successful, but the lesson we can draw from this for life as a whole is that there are no absolutes. There are only options, and options we may have never considered. Being sober was never an option until I put myself in a place in which I felt I had no options.

Had I never had a DUI I do not know if I would be sober today, for better or worse. What I have learned, though, is that you can only gain expertise from practice. Someone overweight who preaches about eating healthy has no platform and is merely a derelict. You should not listen to those who talk about the path but rather those who walk it. The path may not be for you, but as I say, experiment. If there is something inside you that questions something, explore it; you may be surprised by what you find, and your path may change. In my experience it was for the better and has been, not just in sobriety, but in all walks of life.

A bartender's word of advice—"Most of us strive for a life of serenity. In order to be serene, you must believe that a power greater than yourself can help you discern what you can change and what you cannot. If the concept of a power greater than yourself is difficult, step in front of a bus; then you will know a power greater than yourself."

CHAPTER THIRTEEN

Mikey

It was January 2007 when I had come full circle. After nearly a year of being sober and dealing with my DUI requirements, I was faced with the light at the end of what had been a dark tunnel. I had completed 200 hours of community service, my DUI required program, plenty of AA meetings, and now I was faced with my last task to finally put my DUI behind me. I had to go to the Coroner's Office in downtown Los Angeles for their scared-straight type program. We would have to go in and look at the dead bodies as a last reminder of what can happen when me make poor decisions with our lives. By this point I had made it. I had a car again, a solid job, and was working on my dreams with passion. I found myself at rock bottom but had emerged to overcome what was the impossible. I was a success story and not a tragic one.

The scam was almost complete, and after I walked out of this last requirement, I had all intentions of leaving AA and my sobriety behind. I had convinced myself on the drive that I had made a youthful mistake and that despite all I had overcome, it had nothing to do with the changes I had made in my outlook on life and certainly nothing to do with my sobriety. That night I would finally celebrate and reward myself for the hard work I had put in. I was like a fat kid who had gotten slim through hard work and was ready to forget what had worked for him and dive head first into the buffet. However, I would realize that this buffet had dire consequences that had not hit me until that day. I was not going to be scared straight because I was not the one laying on the gurney in the rooms I was about to enter. That wasn't me, and I had done everything on my own—or so I had led myself to believe on that drive.

It took one 30 minute drive to unravel all the insight I had gained over the year and all the lessons I had learned in order to be successful and have a good life. You may have had this moment and fallen back into your old habits rather than embrace the positive changes despite the good fortune they had produced. This is your pride talking, and mine was loud and clear. Then it happened, the moment of clarity that would change my life again in a mere instant.

My cell rang, which was odd because most who knew me realized I would never be awake at eight am, and certainly not on a Saturday. I looked down at the phone, and it was my friend from the program, Ralph, who today is and has been like a big brother to me. He was one of the best friends that I had made since moving to LA and remains as one today. I answered the phone, and Ralph asked me what I was up to. I laughed and told him where I was, not allowing him to know my intentions for the day. When I told him where I was, he fell silent for a moment and then told me of a mutual friend from the program named Mikey.

Mikey reached 10 years sober a few months prior but decided he was in control of his life and would start drinking again. He was 31 and very successful, but I assume he did not attribute his success to his actions of the past 10 years and certainly not to his sobriety.

Ralph said, "I've got some good news. You're going to see him today."

Confused, I asked what he meant.

Ralph said, "Remember how he went out? Well, last night he crashed and killed himself on Culver. "

I don't remember how the call ended, but I was stunned. Shortly after we walked in, the director pointed to three gurneys with body bags.

He pointed to them and said, "This guy died of old age last night, this guy was shot in gang fire, and this guy died in a drunk driving accident."

It was Mikey. I only saw the bag but I knew it was him, and then it finally hit home to me. We make choices every day of our lives, and many seem insignificant, but even those choices can lead us to our deaths.

As I drove home that day I no longer had intentions of drinking that night. I realized that I had been luckier than I had ever realized because that could have easily been me. I could have and maybe should have died that night, but I was spared. I had been placed in a dark tunnel, and my ego told me I came out of it on my own, but this could not be further from the truth. It was being humble and listening to others that had pushed me forward. The willingness to surrender my ego and control over to those who knew a better way was the gift I had been given, not just my life.

This is not a story to scare you or even tell you sobriety is the answer because most of us do not have a problem with drinking. Be aware though that our choices can cause problems, and many of them can cost the ultimate price. What I learned is that I could not pinpoint one exact thing that had brought me from the ashes. I did not have to change a few things, but everything, to find my way in order to value life and suck the marrow out of it.

Upon reflection for me, I realized there was actually one thing that I had done every day no matter what that had led me to this point in my life. That one thing was the decision I made every day not to drink. Now, we can argue that not drinking may not have been the reason I had achieved so much and overcome so many obstacles when the odds were against me, but I counter with this notion: if an athlete wins every contest with the same pair of socks, why would he change them? You can call it superstition, but why risk it? Mikey decided to risk his win streak and change his socks, and for what? He eventually lost and paid the ultimate price. I made it simple for myself. Call me superstitious, but if the formula had worked so well for a year then why change it? So I have made the decision every day to keep that formula and not drink. Some days are good, and some days really suck, but I know that by making this choice, my opportunities have a better success rate. Maybe there is something that you need to decide to do or not do on a daily basis that will steadily improve your life. It could be reading every day, saving five bucks no matter what, eating an apple, whatever it is, commit to it. The scam I was trying to run backfired, and I am so grateful it did. I ran the experiment, and my life got better; had it not I would have ended the experiment. Where you are today you can always return, but if you experiment you may see the opportunity for a greater purpose and outcome for your life.

I do not judge those who drink, and I do not hold myself above them. I do worry about those who drink to excess because I think that they are taking an unneeded risk. I have found that 99 times out of 100 I can drink responsibly, but that one time I fail at it, it creates problems and puts me in situations that could cost me the ultimate price.

That one time out of 100 is not worth it to me, so I make the decision every day not to drink. It is every day, though. I do not make the decision for the rest of my life—today I make the decision just for today.

Approach life with this mindset. I am going to be successful today, I am going to work on my dreams today, I am going to improve myself more TODAY. When we make it larger than it needs to be it becomes too daunting and weighs on us. Every day my life gets a little better, even when it seems like it is not. The girl I like doesn't like me; does that mean my life isn't better? NO. It is because of how I view it. She doesn't like me, GOOD, I can stop wasting my time on her and find someone who does. My boss bagged on me today, today was terrible, NO. Today was progress because now I can work to get better at my job or even motivate myself to find a better job. Every negative is flipped and turned positive because it is an opportunity to learn and grow. Mikey's death, while sad and tragic for me, served a greater purpose. His death kept me from undoing all the positives in my life and reverting back to my old self. I did not drink that night, and every time I even consider it I see his face. I feel sorry for those who loved and missed him, but I benefit from his negative outcome because I learned how important all the choices we make in life are.

Everything we experience in life is neutral, it is our feelings and how we interpret them that dictates whether or not an experience is positive or negative. If I drink tomorrow, did I fail? Will I have instantly forgotten everything I learned over the years? NO. I will have learned that I need to refocus myself in areas so as not to repeat it and avoid failure. I do not have to experiment with drinking anymore because Mikey already did it for me, and his results are good enough for me to draw the conclusion that my life and who I am are better when I am sober. Allow others to fail and learn from their mistakes; it's easier that way.

People challenge me about reading all the books I do about successful people. "You are not them, and you are certainly not at their level, so why bother?" they ask.

Because when I get to their level I will be prepared, and I can get there faster than they did because I have learned from their mistakes and will therefore not make them myself. You do not show up to the championship game without practice and the many games that lead to that day. If you did, you would be certain to fail. It is the ones who have put in the practice day after day, simulations that have prepared them for the championship, who are crowned champions. Championships, success, and growth do not happen overnight; they are won by taking the first step, experimenting with what works and does not, and certainly from learning from those who have come before us. I miss Mikey but carry his spirit with me every day of my life. Maybe you have a Mikey in your life whom you have chosen not to learn from or carry with you in your everyday affairs. You owe it to him and yourself to be the best you can be and live for him. Live the life he chose to leave behind because he made a mistake, a mistake you now benefit from as a lesson.

A bartender's word of advice—"A man fell deep into a pothole and could not get out. A preacher came by and said a prayer for him. The man

*thanked him but pointed out he was still in the hole.
A millionaire came by and wrote him a check and
tossed it to him. Again, he thanked him but was still
stuck in the hole. Later, a stranger came by, looked
down, and jumped in the hole with him. The man
thanked the stranger but pointed out that now they
were both stuck in the hole. The stranger agreed
but told him, ' I have been here before, and I know
the way out. '"*

CHAPTER FOURTEEN

The Barstool Prophets

The bar is full of barstool prophets that pose as visionaries and experts like crows on a fence expelling their "wisdom" whether you have asked for it or not. I have meet thousands of customers over the years and have had many conversations that were truly enlightening. You never know who will come into your life, but like I have said before, if you have an open door you allow the good in with the bad. A barstool prophet is the one who sits there day after day just waiting for his chance to talk. If there is a game on, he knows all there is about the sport and the teams. When you casually mention some difficulty you're having, he knows exactly what to do, and lord help you if you have something good in your life to share because he is right there to play devil's advocate. What the prophet is seeking is attention and to build himself up even if it is at the expense of breaking you down.

On the flip-side, the barstool prophets have their opposites whom we will call the "warriors." They come from afar, usually popping in unexpectedly from time to time. They do not reside day after day on a stool but take their perch in the real world. They come down from that perch to have a bite, and if a stimulating conversation emerges, all the better. They do not waste time with the mundane banter that the prophets try to pull them in with, for they do not have time to waste on what-ifs or hypotheticals that are rooted in opinion and not facts. I cherish the warriors and humor the prophets, for it is my job, and I have no escape from the time I clock in to the time I clock out. My only choice is how I allow the information, good or bad, to affect me.

A man named Victor comes in usually once or twice a month. He is a pilot and pops into LA from time to time and always comes in, to my delight. I always hope that I am not too busy when he shows up because I know that after talking to him I will take something away that is positive and inspiring. He is a man who found his passion in life by flying, and while at one point he may have had dreams of grandeur, he knew himself and followed his passion. In doing so, from all accounts, he has made quite a happy life for himself. He did not need to strive for greatness to be happy because he woke up every day loving what he did and the people around him. I, on the other hand, am different. My job is not my passion although I do enjoy it. I share with him my stories from my past, my plans for the future, and what I am working on currently. He loves it and supportively asks genuine questions and exudes positivity. Like Raymond, he sees something within me that is realistic and not simply fantasy. He knows this because at one point he had a dream of pursing his passion and probably faced the naysayers but did not listen. He persevered and realized his dream. Once someone has done this for themselves they can see it in others and rejoice in their pursuits. He is one of my biggest fans and yet he only sees me sporadically. Why? Because he is living his life, not sitting on a stool dreaming about it or blaming his situation for his short comings.

His opposite is a guy named Bruce. By all accounts Bruce's perception is that he is loved by those he sees at the bar and all who know him. What he does not know is that people shake their heads when he leaves, and while they do not really talk shit about him, they just marvel at a man who thinks he has it all when the overall perception is that his life is full of embellishment and not reality. He retired a few years ago, sold his home for enough to quit his job, and was stoked about his new life in retirement. One day as he sat on his stool like he had for years before when he would find solace after a long day of work, he boasted about how he was getting out of town, gonna live the dream. And he did... for about four months. He packed his stuff up and cruised around the country until one day he showed up again to resume his position among the prophets. He had created and shared this fantasy, but it was not his reality. Years of dreaming about this day had finally come, and yet he did not know how to realize this dream because he had no plan. Winners in life have a plan for everything. It is in the planning that we prepare for the day to come so that when we arrive we can implement and not rely on fate. I have had countless conversations with Bruce and some have been good but most are negative. If I tell him about an idea, he doesn't respond with "good for you" or show support. He points out the flaw in my vision, which is fine, but he has no realistic solution to offer. There is nothing wrong with pointing out a problem as long as you have a viable solution. Anything else is simply being negative, and the psychology of this process is simple. I can't do it or never did it so why would you be able to? That is the mindset that the prophets carry with them, and most do not realize that they have this baggage.

The world is full of prophets that will sit on their perch and cast bolts of lightning to challenge you rather than shower you with rain to grow your crops for the harvest of life. You see, most people think that rain is a bad thing, but it is not. Sure, we've heard the saying "raining on your parade," but when you are in the spring of your life as you prepare your crops you will need rain and sunshine to grow, but lightning will only keep you from being in the field. We must avoid the lightning when it comes but remember that it is only temporary and that tomorrow we can get back to work. If we fear that the lightning will come then we will allow fear to rule our life. I have learned that those who cast these bolts do it simply because they know no other way. They do not know what we know and that is that life is hard, but so what? You couldn't realize your dreams and that's a shame, but I will not allow your shortcomings and negative attitude to keep me from realizing mine. The warriors will shower you, sometimes with praise, but many times with constructive criticism. Their criticism is caution, but they provide a solution or a different perspective while never tearing you down. They will point out flaws in your thinking, and this may make you raw, but their solutions will be the ointment to soothe what you may perceive as lashings. The prophets simply try to tear you down and then put salt in your wounds.

When a topic as simple as sports comes up, which is very common in a bar, these prophets believe they know everything. They watch a lot of sports, but they are not intelligent about the subject because of their bias. I grew up a Duke fan, and to this day I can argue that Christian Laettner was the greatest college basketball player of all time. Many people do not like Duke and even hate Laettner, which is why they will argue all night long and even say that I only think the way I do because of my allegiance to the team. As an intellect, I know that there are plenty of players who were arguably better, such as Walton, Kareem, and Maravich. That is what makes sports so great; there is no definitive way to know who was the best because it's subjective, and when people say that Laettner definitely was not the best, I lose all respect and simply walk away. You cannot argue with ignorance. I can easily see how someone could argue that he was not the best; in fact, I can even argue it. Those who cannot argue against their own beliefs do not truly embrace intelligence.

Sam Walton spent more time in his competitors' stores than in his own! That is the mark of a true intellect and of humility. He knew that he did not know everything and that there were no absolutes in life. He was the greatest businessman of recent history, and yet he was smart enough to know he did not know everything. Take a lesson from Mr. Walton and be the warrior, not the prophet. As I said, I have no choice, I have a commitment to my job to stand there and humor the prophet. However, it is my choice to either allow them to draw me in for their need of debate and attention or not, so I reply, "You have your opinion to which you are entitled," and end the conversation. When I go home I make the choice to realize that I do not have to allow the opinions of others to dictate my life, especially when they are rooted in opinion and not facts.

I wish there were more Victors in my daily interactions behind the bar, and I implore you to be like Victor and not like Bruce. Find your passion and go after it as if your life depended on it, but do it with a plan. Be willing to pivot and accept that you do not know everything, and you will be on your way to a happier life. Many of you are like

Bruce, and it is not your fault. We are taught at an early age that we can be anything, but then we grow older and the majority of people do not realize their childhood dreams. They are thrusted into their own hell in which they have allowed someone else's plan to rule their life. Bruce did everything he believed was the right way in life, and the majority of society would even pat him on the back for his efforts. He worked hard, reached a place of retirement, and in the harvest of his life, he found that the crops he had cultivated were not as great as he had dreamed. The worst part is that he did not know even what to do with them.

Years ago before I was a bartender, I would sit on my barstool as a sportscaster over my pint with a dream to one day be at a place in my life at which I could drink all day and play golf. This sounds like a great dream to many. As I have moved forward in my life more than 10 years removed from those days. I now realize how shallow and unambitious of a dream that really was. The purpose of life is growth, and at that time my purpose was to get to a point where I no longer grew. How ridiculous that sounds to me now. Hell, I don't even love golf. Why did I have that dream?

Well, it was simple; I had no real plan and no vision. It sounded good, and it was a sound that echoed from a thousand generations of voices telling me that that was what you did when you retired. One of my mentors is now retired and plays golf almost every day. He loves the game, and it gives him a reason to wake up in the morning. But that is only ONE reason he gets up because his day is filled working with others to help them realize their potential and with being a great husband and grandfather. Look at the contrast to his reality

201

versus my old dream. I wanted to only have two reasons to wake up in retirement: to play a game I don't really love because it seemed like that's what I was supposed to do and then to drink all day and waste away. What kind of life would that be?

The reason Bruce goes to the bar every day before it even opens is because he could not find a greater purpose in life. He has created this notion in his head that he has to report to the bar every day like a job. Now, certainly it's easier for him to show up at the bar than to work, but is that really what you want your purpose to be? If it is, great, you have chosen a very attainable goal and should have no problem realizing it, but if you want more, then get your pen and paper out and start formulating your destiny.

We all have something within us that wants to be immortal and leave a legacy behind. What will yours be? Have you even given it much thought? The easiest way to be immortal is to bear a child with your name. Then your DNA and genetic makeup will hopefully last a few generations long after you have left this existence. I envy those who seemingly have no desire and are not concerned with this idea of a legacy or immortality. The truth is that there are very few who truly do not consider this. My father is one, but what is ironic is that while he is not concerned with this notion he will still leave a legacy, and his immortality will go on after he dies at the very least through me. His legacy will also continue since he is a professor. His legacy will likely be short lived but will carry on after he dies because of his effect on his students. The lessons he has passed on will be shared to a generation to come after he has passed.

Is it a legacy like Alexander the Great?

Of course not, but nonetheless it is a legacy. I wonder what Bruce's legacy will be because he has put so much stock in the wrong areas. He feels value when he shows up to the bar, but when he passes maybe some will talk about him for a year or two but soon he will fade into the dust, and no one will know his name when he is gone. This may sound very harsh, but I just want you to think about it and reflect on your own life—when you die, if you could review it, would you be happy with it? Bruce may very well be happy with his life, and that's great, but I would not be happy with his life, and so I strive for a higher purpose and a greater legacy than simply being known as a hard worker and a regular at a bar.

In the film *Troy*, Achilles is faced with the decision to go to Troy and fight.

He confronts his mother before he makes his final decision, and she tells him, "If you stay here you will be happy, marry, and have children who love you. When you have passed on to the next life your children will speak of you to their children and their children will speak of you to the next generation, but then you will be forgotten. However, if you go to Troy, your name will be remembered throughout history, and you will be revered."

I remember watching this scene and saying to myself, "Yes, I will go to Troy."

Now, I have no delusions that people will be speaking of me a thousand years from now; however, I do want to leave my mark on this world. I am doing this right now by writing this book. If I win a world title in poker I will be forever etched into the history books. Granted, my legacy will not be that of those such as Twain, Poe, or Doyle

Brunson, but when I find myself in my last moments in life, I want to make damn sure that I am leaving this Earth with a list that is completely exhausted.

We cannot allow others to rent space in our heads and tell us why we cannot do something. We have to use this as fuel to push forward and create our legacy in life that is greater than we could ever imagine. My father probably does not even realize the impact he has had on the thousands of students he has taught over the years. Every once in a while he runs into a student years later who tells him how he changed their life. When he is gone there will still be students who feel that way and recall the lessons he passed on. Even better, they will use his lessons on their children who will in turn hopefully pass them on to their own. You too can have this kind of impact. You too can take your last breath knowing that you left no stone unturned and that you made a difference in this world that will echo throughout generations to come.

As Henry Thoreau said, "Most people live a life of quiet desperation." They are simply trying to get by and have the wrong mentality, but you do not have to be like this. I love bartending for so many reasons that I have shared with you, but the greatest gift is that I get to learn from all walks of life on a daily basis. I learn how not to be like Bruce the prophet and how to be a warrior like Victor. Both come to the same bar, enjoy the same environment, yet they look and experience the world completely differently. Like anything in life, moderation is key. I love cookies, but I cannot live off them alone. What is fascinating is that if I ate only cookies I would grow to dislike them. Spending every day in the bar, I really question if those prophets really enjoy their visits as much as Victor. I don't believe they do, and that's because they are living in a self-induced fantasy world rather than making their fantasies a reality. I always say that life's problems are solved every night by the bar prophets; many are actually smart, however, but they forget their solutions because they are too drunk to remember what they discovered. I see people every day working on their dreams in the bar, coffee shops, or parks. Maybe subconsciously these people are surrounding themselves by others who motivate them. If they look over at the guy smashing the keys on his laptop they will be inspired to stop daydreaming and get to work. In the bar, the prophets do not create this positive motivation but a negative one that says, "Take it easy, have another beer, there is always tomorrow."

A few times a year I go to skid row in downtown LA and speak on a panel in front of the lowest forms of life you can imagine. The homeless, drug users, prostitutes, you name it. People ask me why I do it. At first it seems like I am doing a good deed, but overwhelmingly most people think that I am wasting my time because these people are hopeless. I even feel sometimes that when I speak no one is listening and that my efforts are for naught. There are times when this is true and that no matter how inspiring or compelling my words may be, they fall on deaf ears. However, there may be one person who listens, and for that reason it is worth it. It is not a true act of altruism though. I do it for myself just as much. I do it because when I am down there on skid row I can see what happens when someone doesn't have a plan for life or their plan took a hit and they did not prepare themselves to pivot around obstacles. I also do it because when

I am of service I am at my best. I am the best
person I can be because I am willing to put aside
myself in order to be available for others.

One of the greatest business persons of our time
was Mother Teresa. Yes, she was, and you
probably never even conceived that idea. How
could I say that considering she died without a dime
to her name? Certainly she was probably the most
caring and selfless person in our recent history, but
why would I say she was a great business person?
She was a master at raising capital, although it was
not for her personal gain; nonetheless, her service
was one to emulate. Every opportunity she was
faced with in life she thought of how she could be
of service and capitalize her efforts for the greater
good. Her business was helping others, and her
abilities are comparable to the savvy CEO on the
Forbes list.

Late in her life she was in need of surgery,
and without it she would likely die. Obviously she
had no insurance and certainly no money, but
because of who she was, she had the top doctors in
the world lined up to help her. Not many people in
this world can have this kind of impact, but what
she did with this opportunity and how she
capitalized on it is a lesson we can learn from. With
all these doctors lined up, she flew to San Diego to
meet with them all. Nearly 50 doctors were willing
to lend their services, but before she would meet
with any of them she made them all sign a contract
that would have them spend time giving free health
relief to an area in Mexico that sorely needed it.
She was facing death and yet still managed to
optimize the situation for a greater good. They all
signed the contact, and she made it successfully
through her surgery. Regardless of her own fate,

though, she would have helped hundreds of others even if she had passed away. Her legacy, like my father, was not a concern for her, but her actions created an immortal legacy that would affect others after she left this earth. Certainly her name will echo throughout history, and while we all cannot be like her, we can learn from her and strive to live by her example.

Perception is the key. You may perceive Mother Teresa as simply a loving, selfless modern-day saint, but now I have challenged that perception and shown you how great she was at business. You have also seen a different perception of business; it is not just Wall Street and big corporations. Your life is a business, and you are the CEO. Now I ask you, what is your perception of your own life? Are you the prophet sitting on your self-assumed stool, the warrior who moderates the simple pleasures of life while indulging in his true pleasures and passions, or are you at a crossroads? The truth is that we are always at a crossroads. The prophet can pivot and become the warrior, and the warrior can regress and become the prophet. In the end, what will your legacy be? Will you be able to take that final breath and say, yes, I did it the best I could, and I can now leave this earth without regret?

A bartender's word of advice—"It is easy to rely on fate to determine our lives. It is easier to believe that we have no control and are slaves to our destiny. It is our choice to sit on the couch waiting for fortune to arrive, and so if we have a choice to sit then we also have a choice to stand. This choice smashes any notion of a predetermined destiny, so in reality our destiny is induced by our own creation through our own choices. Stand and deliver your destiny, for this is your true fate."

CHAPTER FIFTEEN

Stories of the Bar and Inspirations

Working for over a decade behind the bar has shown me so many lessons in life that I have shared with you. The reason the bar is such a magnificent lab for the study of human nature is that everyone goes there on many occasions. The social aspect draws us all in, and the social distraction keeps others within the self-constructed comfort it assumes. I have given multiple examples of whom you may be and whom you can become. It is up to you to make the ultimate decision to where you will place yourself in this microcosm of society. The gift of human interactions has probably kept me in this line of work longer than I should have stayed. It is not simply the golden handcuffs but the ease of living that it provides as well. I am able to get paid to learn from others and be social. Every profession has elements of social interaction, but in the bar I am paid and encouraged to be social, whereas in most professions this can be a distraction. These social interactions have molded me into who I am today, taking positive notes from some and lessons of what not to do and avoid from others. One of the reasons patrons look to the bartender is because of all the experiences we are privileged to endure.

I've mentioned a few of the different types of people I have come in contact with and how they have taught me life lessons from every aspect of life. I recall a pivotal moment in my life after Katrina. While I was bartending at a country club in my hometown and filled with despair and self-pity despite my goal of moving to LA being set, I found myself in a truly character testing position. The holiday season was in full swing, and I had to work a Christmas party. I did not think anything of it other than it would be another day at work and one more step toward my goal. This party was different. It was a party that included a number of my childhood acquaintances whom I had resented since the day I left my hometown for college. I had envisioned coming back to my hometown one day and showing everyone how much better I was, riding a chariot of success and notoriety.

Despite all the positive things I had accomplished to that point in my life, my reality was that I was serving them drinks while they were leading what I believed to be successful lives. Once again, I felt "less than," and worse, in front of the very people I wanted so badly to show up. I swallowed my pride and did my job to the best of my abilities, and something unexpected happened. They were not the jerks of privilege I had created them to be. Some were doing well, and others were struggling just like I was to find their ways in life. As the party winded down, there were two guys whom I had strong resentments toward who lingered while I was cleaning up.

Chris was everything I wanted to be in high school, and I had known him growing up. He was a top athlete, smart, and came from a wealthy family. He had it all: the girl, the looks, and he seemingly got everything he ever wanted. As we caught up and I told him my story he shared his with me. He had gotten a good job, made a good living, and married his high school sweetheart. It made sense I thought; he of course had it all, but this was my perception and not his reality. He told me how he was having to move to Atlanta because his wife had gotten a great job, and he had to follow her career.

Astounded, I could see the disappointment in his face. Here was my definition of the alpha male having to take a back seat for his wife. I used to believe that I wanted his life, but as he told me his story I realized that I did not want it at all because I was different.

He was taking the path that he felt he should, but it was not what he wanted. In fact, he was more interested in my story and admitted he was jealous. The tables had turned, and he was envious of my life and where it had taken me and my vision of what I was pursuing. He envied my life, and I now realized that I actually did not want to be him and was perfectly fine with who I was. I used this encounter to help open my eyes. I was living a life that few people, even the Chrises of the world, had the courage to live.

Everyone dreams of taking the road less traveled, but very few do. While they can easily rationalize their choices, deep down, they knew they did not have the courage I exuded and had been living. You see how perception is not reality. I am living a life few can so that I can have the life they never will. Chris may very well end up a happy, wealthy man. His bank account may far exceed mine when it is all said and done, but I wonder now, will his happiness exceed mine? Happiness is not a competition because the only score that is kept and matters is the one you keep with yourself. We ended our conversation with him hoping that I would reach out to him and visit in Atlanta. He even told me that if I ever needed a place to crash I was welcome. Amazing, I had held on to a resentment that may have kept me from having a friendship in our youth. As it turns out, this was a great gesture. I never took him up on his offer because I had my own path to blaze, but I am humbled by it to this day. I try my best to never carry resentments because you never know what positives you may be missing due to your negative attitude toward another, simply out of jealousy.

Another guy there that night was named Tyler. Now, I was never jealous of Tyler, but he was from a seemingly wealthy family who always bailed him out. He was short and not that smart, mostly because he was a slacker, and his family even helped him get into college. I always felt I was better than him, certainly as a person, but I was jealous of his place in society. When we spoke I could see that the reason we never got along was because he was jealous of ME! I would have never believed this had he not admitted it. It could have been a few too many drinks, but I was surprised, and when I caught him up on my life, all he could say was, "Man, I always knew you would do big things."

"How could he say that?" I thought as I served him drinks. He was even jealous of me as a bartender. He understood the money that I was making and certainly the girl factor that comes with the job. He was looking for work and had previously taken a job that his family had helped him get but lost or quit for whatever reason. He was still living at home doing what he had been doing years ago. I do not know what ever came of Tyler, and we left the conversation cordially, but just like Chris I found an opportunity to grow within myself. We believe that others have it better than us or are lucky because of their birth rite. Some are given a head start, but that does not mean they are prepared for the race of life. The greatest takeaway from these two encounters was that I found that I was right where I was supposed to be. I needed to stop competing with others because I can always find those I am ahead of or behind. What truly matters is the competition within. Am I competing as hard as I can versus my expectations and my self-doubt? When I lie down at night and feel that I have taken at least one step forward and not allowed resentments or self-doubt to push me back then I can rest easy knowing that I am on my way.

When I was working at The Waterfront I had two other bartenders whom I shared the busy nights with. One was Kurt, who at the time was actually the head bartender. He was great and a good friend. We made a lot of money together, but one day he was let go, and I was moved forward to his title of head bartender. Kurt, the other bartender, was just like the guy who wakes up and does just enough to survive. He had ambition but not a lot, and he never acted upon it. He actually had a role in a major film purely by chance, and he could have easily used it as a spring board, but he did not have the passion to do so nor the drive for something greater with his life at the time. He was content with his job and the money he made. He enjoyed concerts, travel, and taking advantage of all of life's luxuries.

When he was let go, however, after months of half-halfheartedly trying to find a job, he ran out of money and had to move back home. His tale is not tragic but one that occurs when one is comfortable rather than driven. In this day and age the rug can be swept out from under you like it was for him, and then you may find that you are not prepared for the discomfort and must retreat. He ended up finding a good job back home and is back to his comfortable life. I think that for him this is just fine, and he will live his live in contentment, and there is nothing wrong with that. I use it as motivation because that is not good enough for me. We worked side-by-side, but I chose to seize the opportunity, and for me that has made a difference. We may have been cut from similar cloth, but we are folded and utilized differently. To be honest, I am envious of his outlook on life because it is much easier to pursue than the one I have chosen. I know that I would not be able to sleep at night if I had his outlook, and that is my issue that I deal with and what keeps me striving and working for more.

Kurt was replaced by a guy named Kevin. Kevin was a local and somewhat equal to Kurt as far as a coworker and outlook on life. I remember working with him when he got the annoying question bartenders despise.

"So what do you do?"

My ear perked up because I knew he had nothing going on other than this job and he was just trying to make a living, so I was curious as to how he would handle this question.

He laughed and said, "What do you mean? I work full time here. It's where I grew up."

They persisted, as they do, and said, "You mean you have never lived anywhere else?"

"No way, why would I? The weather is great, my friends are here, there's no better place to be."

I couldn't agree with him more; LA to me is the top of the mountain. I have lived in a number of cities, and I can honestly admit that I would never want to live anywhere else. I feel at home here because it has everything I could ever want. People counter with the traffic issue or cost of living, but I laugh at that. If traffic is that big of a deciding factor in your life then you have greater issues, my friend. Obviously it is not cheap to live here, but look what you get for your money. The weather is perfect, I am a five-minute walk from the beach, it boasts some of the most beautiful people in the world and many of the most successful people, plus the opportunities are endless. If those are the only two arguments you have against living in LA, then maybe you should look at your plan and not your circumstance. I know that LA is not for everyone, but I want to surround myself with winners, and this is one of the meccas for that.

As far as Kevin is concerned, his reasons were just as viable. I realized that how he handled that question was way better than me being filled with resentment or seeing those who asked as challengers. I try not to get upset with that question now, and in return I am a happier person for it. Kevin's life, much like Chris', is not one I would like to emulate, but they are seemingly content, which makes me happy for them both—it's just not for me. What I can't understand, which brings me to the lesson that I have learned from Kevin, is how he can be where he is when we work side-by-side. We made roughly the same amount of money, yet he could never pay his bills on time and was always broke. On the flip side, I always paid my bills ahead of time and became a homeowner. Now, certainly the poker helped with that a bit, but he could easily have a life without quiet desperation. He chose to be pennywise and dollar foolish, and he is one rug sweep away from falling on his face. He is dependent on his wage when he should focus on a profit. When one's wages cease they are in despair, while the one who has profit can weather the storm.

I learned how not to conduct my finances from

Kevin. Our society has a YOLO mentality: You Only Live Once. I like this motto and apply it, but there circumstances for which it should be avoided. For all of us, those situations vary, but the mistake we make with this motto is that we use it in all aspects, in all moments. You only live once means you should seize the opportunities of life as a whole and not have a narrow vision. Everyday Kevin may enjoy the day better than I, but when the storm comes it will wipe him out far worse than it will for me.

Do not live in fear of the storm; it will come, just prepare. I recall a story someone once told me one day while I was behind the bar about Katrina and God. A man was facing Katrina and was hell-bent on standing his ground, saying God would help him. As the rains came, a policeman came by and offered him help to leave, and he said, "No, God will take care of me."

As the water rose, a man in a boat paddled up to him and offered him a ride, to which he responded, "No, God is going to help me."

Finally, the water reached so high he was forced to stand on his roof, when a helicopter came by, but again he refused, saying God would take care of him.

The man finally drowned. and when he reached the pearly gates, he asked God," I believed in you with all my heart that you would help me and you left me to die; how could you do this to me?"

God responded," I sent you help three times, and you denied it; what more could I have done?"

This hit home so hard for me. This idea of YOLO, everything will be okay is fool's gold, and we must abolish it. We all need help, and we all need to prepare and not rest on the idea that everything happens for a reason and that we are simply the result of our fate. Everything does happen for a reason, but we do have some control over it, and preparing and being humble will allow us to navigate the storm, seek refuge, and regroup so that when we fall, we fall forward, and are able to get back up. Most of us will endure the storm, and, honestly, we will all likely survive, but how we come out on the other side is up to us.

Changing gears now, I recall a time in New Orleans when I had a night that was one for the record books involving a girl. I was bartending a slow day shift, and it was a scorcher of a day in which the humidity felt like a sauna. As I was ending my shift, an older couple, a gentleman, and a beautiful young lady saddled up to the bar. The girl was the daughter of the couple, and the other gentleman was her uncle. We had exchanged stories, and my interest in the girl, Hanna, was apparent. As I finished up my shift, they invited me to have one last drink with them before I left. They were from England, and I shared with them my stories while they obliged with their own. They were on holiday and had frequented the city over the years and fell in love with it. At one moment, the father excused himself to assist the uncle with his travel arrangements back at the hotel, as the uncle was leaving that evening.

I stayed with the two ladies and continued our conversation when Hanna excused herself to the ladies room. Her mother leaned in and shared with me that Hanna had taken a liking to me. Excited, I told her that I too liked her, and when Hanna joined us we kept our secret but shared knowing glances amid the conversation. Shortly after the father returned, he was pleased to see I was still in their company. He asked me to join them for dinner, and we dined at one of the top restaurants the city had to offer, enjoying a five-course meal. I cannot recall our conversations, but what I remember most was how these strangers had welcomed me, and our connection as a whole was truly enjoyable through every moment we shared. When the bill came I reached for my wallet only to be denied by the father. After the bill was returned he slid the credit card to his daughter and said, "Go and enjoy this fine evening with Jason; I am sure you two will have a memorable night."

Probably the best bait-and-switch/wingman move I have ever encountered. I had not tried to win them over with anything out of character and was true to myself. It was good enough to win the approval of her parents, whom I could tell had a major influence on her. As we left, I showed her around the city, and we enjoyed the night only to find ourselves at the river bank on a park bench. We both had butterflies but shared a true YOLO moment. We leaned in for a kiss that touched every cell in my body from head to toe. We continued our embrace until a security guard told us crazy kids we had to move on because the park was closed. As I walked her back with my feet feeling like they barely made contact with the earth, we arrived at her hotel. We kissed goodnight, and to this day I have never seen Hanna or her family again. Hanna and I emailed but lost touch despite my romantic mind telling me we would one day reunite.

This was a true YOLO moment. I could have made so many decisions that were safe or polite or maybe even the right thing to do, but I would have missed out on a magical night. It was something more that only happens to those who truly throw caution to the wind and say, why not? I don't pretend to believe this was a norm; though it was certainly an anomaly, what are the true pleasures in life if not a queue of anomalies? Be true to yourself, and others will embrace it if you are genuine. Be humble enough to accept invitations because I certainly could have stopped while I was ahead, but I wouldn't have the story to share with you or even this one that I can fondly remember. Would it have made a better ending if Hanna and I found a way to see each other again and more so have a life together? Maybe. This is not how the story was meant to end, but it is the way that our stories in life manifest in reality, not fantasy. Fantasize about the future, but be willing to pivot and take the road less traveled because in this story, it made all the difference.

The last tale from the bartender memoirs I will share is one that is not defining but actually common. We will have our peaks and valleys that will shape our lives and influence them, but the common ones are what create who we are based on how we approach them and embrace them. Again, this tale is about a girl, this time named Janice. I met her one evening and was immediately impressed with her beauty, and through our interactions during my service I found she was truly compelling. Every topic I opened with she had an intellectual take on, some of which challenged me while others complemented my views. She was with a friend whom I did not neglect based on the knowledge I gathered over the years of approach. I knew that her friend's approval and acceptance was just as important because when I was attending to other duties she could easily influence Janice in her opinion of me. When they closed out and said good bye, I came from behind the bar and asked for her number. She smiled but informed me that she does not give her number out at bars. I could have felt rejected, which would be understandable; however, I appreciated this because it was not me that she was rejecting per se but the environment. I also looked at it as a challenge on the off chance I would see her again.

She came in a month or so later, and I simply talked to her but refrained from asking for her number. It was not the right move and would look too persistent. My strategy was to build rapport so that the next time I could make my move. She had also had proven that she would likely return. A month went by when she appeared again, and once again, she was with a friend. I ignored her at first, but noticed she was looking my way more often, and it was noticeable. I decided to make my move and engage her. Being sure to engage her friend, we talked, and I slid in the fact that I did magic. Like I assumed, they wanted to see it, but I denied them at first. I allowed the appeal to build up and then before they were to leave, I told them to cash out and I would do some magic for them. When the time had come I did not do it on their turf but brought them to a table away from the crowd and employed a few tricks, ending with my connection trick. It went over well, and when I was done, I told them it was a pleasure seeing them and wished them well.

As they rose to leave, I cut them off and said to Janice, "I know your rule about not giving your number in the bar, so we can go outside, and I can ask you again, or you can give it to me now. I've already proven we have a connection, and I can read your mind, so we should just save time. You can put it into my phone that's right here."

She smiled, grabbed my phone, and inputted her number, saying she looked forward to hearing from me. As they left, I returned to my duties when a guy approached me who unknowingly had been watching intently throughout the process.

He said," Jason, you are my hero. I just watched the whole thing and you just got the number of the hottest girl I have ever seen in this bar. How the hell did you do that?"

I smiled and said, "I knew what I wanted, and what I was worthy of getting, and I prepared for the moment so that I wouldn't let the opportunity pass me by."

He shook his head and said, "Man, you're my role model; I have so much to learn."

The story ends there because it was not about the outcome to follow or even the approval of others but the lesson in preparation and study that is most important with getting girls but more so in getting what we want in life. The prize was not getting the girl or whatever prize you may be striving for, but it is the person you become and how you get there that is the true gift.

A bartender's word of advice—"Every man who is searching for the greatest gifts in life should look no further than the tale of the Alchemist. The miles we endure and the obstacles we face in our search, while beneficial, are of no matter until you realize that the greatest gift is within yourself. If you know yourself then you will find greatness within, and it will shine upon this world, and the reflection will allow you to realize the ultimate gift that you were searching for."

CHAPTER SIXTEEN

Last Call

You walked into my virtual bar when you started this book, and by now you have probably realized this isn't exactly what you were expecting. For better or worse the course of this path we have been on took twists and turns that you may not have foreseen. This was my intention because this is how life is and how every bar experience works. You walk in with one intention and find yourself leaving with your plan deviated. We have had so many talking points, and pivoting has been prevalent. In life, the ones who are successful in all areas are those who pivot. The girl you first saw in the bar isn't the one you spent your time with; the guys you met up with end up going their own way as you explore other opportunities, be it the girl you approached or someone so interesting that you couldn't leave the conversation. Maybe you decided tonight just wasn't for you and retired early. Some of these pivots were for good and bad, but nonetheless, any plan you had most likely does not take course the way you had envisioned. Now you can recognize these opportunities and flourish.

You may be confused as to why a simple activity of going out to the bar would lead to flourishing. Every opportunity and experience we have in life can take two roads, one that moves us forward and one that wastes our time. Sure, there are times when you will go out for a drink to take the edge off, but your plan changes without your knowing, and you are standing there at last call drunk and scrambling. This is where a plan with good intentions was lost, and now you have no plan on how to get home, to get that girl, or what your next move is. Be careful because this is where mistakes are made. This is where you decide a cab isn't worth it and you can take a gamble driving yourself home, or the girl that is left at the bar seems good enough to take home only to wake up the next morning with a sense of regret. I have made these decisions myself, so I know how easy they are to make, but I am telling you to avoid them at all costs because in the end they do not benefit you. When you have a higher pursuit you should not jeopardize it. You may counter with, "It is only one night, one poor decision, only one." Well, what is an ocean but a multitude of drops? It is the "one times" that add up and derail us, and I don't want that for you.

I want you to go to the bar and stay true to yourself and your purpose. There are plenty of solid reasons to go to the bar: socializing, opposite sex pursuits, and relaxing with good food and a beverage. Keep those reasons pure, and do not allow yourself to be swayed in your reasons. When we are not focused we are open to persuasion, and typically it is not for our own benefit. If we are focused, we can allow ourselves to be persuaded judiciously and filter out the bad directions and opinions from the good. Most of us want more out of life than we are willing to admit to others, but deep down in our own self-talk we hear it constantly pushing us to be better. We tend to lower the volume because it makes us uncomfortable, and when we do, the negative self-talk takes over and tells us we can't do it or that we can wait until tomorrow. There is no tomorrow, and I am sure you have heard that before, but it is true. Every aspect of our life should be reviewed and thought out because if it is not benefiting us and where we want to go, everything else is and will take away from us and render negative consequences.

While writing this book I was trying to constantly think of how I would interpret these words from your standpoint and asked myself why it would seem important for me to be sharing all these ideas as opposed to keeping it simple with a bunch of funny bar stories. I want you to benefit from not just knowing the sociology of the bar from my perspective but also from learning the reasons and psychology of why things are the way they are based on those perceptions. Many of the conversations I have with patrons tend to include many of the lessons, advice, and suggestions that I have shared with you. I feel that most who come to the bar may not be directly looking for this insight but through their inquiries they are. Now you have a foundation and can find yourself and where you stand in the social hierarchy I have presented. Now you can decide where you choose to move along this ladder. If you are content being the barstool prophet, then by all means continue as long as you are truly happy. If you want to strive to be the warrior, then get to work if you're not already there.

I want you to become the best you possibly can, and when you sit at my bar many of you are not there yet and express desires to be more. I am here to help, and while at the bar many times the patrons will leave inspired, by the time they arrive to their homes the inspiration has faded and they resort back to their comfort in sitting on their butts.

I want you to be a tree, as Jim Rohn said, "How big does a tree grow? As big as it possibly can!"

Trees do not have will, so they drive their roots

as deep as they will go and spread their branches as far as they can reach because they only know one thing in life, to grow. We have free will, which allows us to grow as far as we can, but we have the constant decision not to. If you can smash this way of thinking and believe that every day you are growing like a tree, you will find what you're looking for in life, be it success, love, and even happiness. This is the true motivation in life that makes it worth living.

"What can happen to one, can happen to all," was shared by Seneca thousands of years ago.

The bar is filled with those, and maybe even you, who think they can't live the life they have the potential to live because other people have it better. This couldn't be further from the truth. The difference is that those who choose to wait until tomorrow are left behind by those who embrace today. I am so proud of a guy like Joe, whom I mentioned earlier. I am not proud because he made it; hell, I will probably never know if he ever made his dreams a reality. What I am proud of is that he made a decision to move from the comfortable path that was dictated by others. Even if he falls back into this mindset he will always be able to look back at that moment he took a chance at happiness and challenged the voices of a thousand generations telling him he was crazy. Should he fall back he will at least be able to look back with confidence at the one time he went for it, and maybe that memory will inspire him to refocus if he regresses.

Aristotle said, "No great intellect has been without a touch of madness."

People think I am crazy, but just as many thought Steve Jobs, Richard Branson, and Martin Luther King, Jr. were as well. That is a small sample of the company you will belong to should you decide today to pursue a life filled with passion and belief. This is a group I would rather align myself with, crazy or not, compared to the 9-to-5ers who are grinding their way, living a life that is "smart" and "secure." I have encountered plenty of people who challenge the way I think and can attack all the ideas and visions I have. I am not a robot, and, yes, that does affect me at times, but it doesn't rule me. I listen and discard as soon as I can because why would they understand what I am doing? It goes against all their fears and reservations. If you want theirs to be yours, listen to them and give them stock, but realize you have just allowed someone else's limiting beliefs to rule over your own.

Some would say, "You are just a bartender; what makes you think you know everything?"

I am the first to admit that I do not know everything and that I am actually looking for someone to challenge my beliefs so that I can learn more. Those who present problems without solutions are not the ones to listen to. My mentors do not do this and constantly point out flaws in my thinking but instantly present new ideas and concepts backed with encouragement to foster better, solid ideas. These are the ones you want around you, not the naysayers without solutions. We are all at different places and times in our life. There are plenty of people who come up to me and are envious of my life.

The kid working at the pizza place across the street listens to me because he knows I am ahead of him in life, and he sees my new car and confidence in social situations and wishes he could be me. The guy who works a desk job is envious of the amount of travel I do and the lifestyle I lead because to him it seems like I am truly enjoying life while he is stuck behind a desk, even though it seems like he has a better career trajectory. He may be working on a career, but he is missing out on life as it passes him by while doing something he really isn't passionate about.

On the other end of the spectrum, though, are those who are ahead of me. These are the ones who are doing what I want to do, and the irony is that they visit the bar very rarely. The ones I am looking up to like the pizza boy looks up to me are not wasting time, they are hustling. So when I get home from work I don't rest, I grind. I am working on the next path.

You don't like your job?

Then bust your ass when you're not at work to get a new one.

I enjoy my job, but I don't want a job, I want something more; and so I work on it as if it is my job. Take that approach to your future: treat it like a job not a hobby. The difference is, if it's what you really want to do and have passion for it, it will never feel like a job. When I am on my grind I cannot stop. I go without sleep constantly because it fuels me. Sometimes you will be discouraged and think that you are a victim of your circumstance and that there is nothing you can do; you're crazy for thinking you can do something you deem as great. The Wright brothers were certainly crazy in their time, and to believe that they could make man fly was insane, but they pushed through the many obstacles with no encouragement. Once they broke through, look how quickly flight escalated. In 1903 man first flew and by 1969 he had landed on the moon.

Think of any obstacle you have and how difficult it is, and ask yourself, "Is it harder than solving the problem of landing a man on the moon?"

If it is not, and I am sure it isn't, then you can do it. Maybe you can't figure out the path on your own. Surround yourself with those who can help you. Neil Armstrong didn't land on the moon by himself; there were plenty of highly-trained brains collaborating for this goal, which is one reason why I believe he says, "This is one small step for man, one giant leap for mankind."

He took the step but it was mankind that put him there and would benefit. When you think in these terms, the universe will get out of the way and it will be up to you to make it happen.

What will be your legacy? I wake up every day and ask myself this question. Some days it is clear, and other days I need to sharpen the iron of my sword a bit more.

Seneca said, "Often, a very old man has no proof of his life than his age."

Just because you live long doesn't mean you have truly lived and doesn't make you an expert on life. It just means you have managed to survive.

Is that what you want, just to survive?

If you do, I can promise you that you will not get out alive. I don't think you want to wake up when you are old and feeble and say, wow, I managed to get here. There is no prize to win by living long. The prize comes from living fully. We want to get to the end and say, I left everything on the court of life and gave it my all. When I first thought of writing this book I thought it would be about poker and winning the big title. I could write about the path and struggle and how it all worked out and paid off in the end. I didn't realize that the true success was not the end result but the path. I may never win a world title in poker or achieve the greatness I dream of, but that does not mean I was unsuccessful. The true success is that I made the decision not to listen to those filled with fear and blinded by false security. I know that when the curtain falls on my life I will meet it knowing that I never had a desire in my life that I did not explore. I have been a bartender, sportscaster on TV, an actor in Hollywood, an award winning magician,a poker professional, and now CEO of my own company.

Now I am the Bartending Therapist helping others realize that the pursuit is more powerful than the goal. It is the learning and mindset that says I will go for it that is the gift because taking the road less traveled will always make the difference, whether we get to the destination we originally envisioned or pivoted to something greater. For me, I now realize that my original trajectory was not my destiny but a multitude of experiences for others to learn from in order to realize the need to find their own true potential. I am the guinea pig that went through the tests and endured the hardships all so that I could tell you it was worth it. I could be viewed as simply a bartender; what can I possibly offer other than cold drinks? But just like the guy who challenged me to get sober, inspiration doesn't come from a title, it comes from someone who touches a nerve. I am not defined by any title I have ever held or how I pay my bills but by my character and life experiences. I hope that I have done that and helped you realize that greatness lies within you and that it has lain dormant long enough. Now is the time to unleash your greatness and take

your place upon the shoulders of the giants that
came before you.

Made in the USA
Las Vegas, NV
26 July 2021